THE Mile End COOKBOOK

THE
Mile End
COOKBOOK

REDEFINING JEWISH COMFORT FOOD
FROM HASH TO HAMANTASCHEN

NOAH & RAE BERNAMOFF

WITH MICHAEL STOKES & RICHARD MAGGI

Clarkson Potter/Publishers
New York

MELCHER
MEDIA

Library of Congress Cataloging-in-Publication Data | Bernamoff, Noah. | The Mile End cookbook : redefining Jewish comfort food, from hash to hamantaschen / Noah and Rae Bernamoff ; with Michael Stokes & Richard Maggi. -- 1st ed. | p. cm. | Includes index. | ISBN 978-0-307-95448-0 | eISBN 978-0-307-95449-7 | 1. Jewish cooking. 2. Comfort food. I. Bernamoff, Rae. II. Stokes, Michael. III. Maggi, Richard. IV. Title. | TX724.B4646 2012 | 641.5′676--dc23 | 2012013467

Printed in China | 10 9 8 7 6 5 4 3 2 1 | First Edition

FOR NANA LEE & GRANDMA BEA—
OUR ENDURING SOURCES
OF WISDOM AND INSPIRATION

Contents

Clockwise, from top left: Noah and Rae; the deli;
Chicken Soup

Preface

I DIDN'T KNOW IT AT THE TIME, but the night I met Noah—in the spring of 2003, seven years before we opened our Brooklyn restaurant, Mile End—he was wearing his grandfather's shirt. That should have told me a lot. All I was aware of at that moment, though, was that the shirt in question was kind of loud, and the guy wearing it was making a very convincing argument against the existence of God. Not a particularly radical point of view in a dorm room at McGill University in Montreal, except that this was a Shabbat dinner, where we were supposed to be getting back in touch with our spirituality.

What I soon realized about Noah, and what made me feel connected to him right away, was that spirituality for him had little to do with doctrine and devout belief and everything to do with history, ritual, tradition, and family—and also a fierce intellectual curiosity. All are qualities that put him in good company with other notable self-questioning Jews through the ages, and with me. We'd both grown up in somewhat lapsed kosher households—he in Montreal and I in New York City and northern New Jersey—and had loving parents who'd sent us to parochial school in hopes of putting us right with the Torah and traditional teachings. For both me and Noah, all that strict schooling had backfired slightly, awakening in us a restless and skeptical spirit.

Suffice it to say that Noah and I hit it off. Before long, I was making regular trips with him to his parents' house in the suburbs of Montreal, where his family was never not eating. A pickle plate was always out, and salami and sausages and steaks were on the grill more often than not, no matter the weather. Between meals, the fridge door opened and closed with a metronomic regularity. And then there were his Nana Lee's prodigious Friday-night dinners—more about her on the following pages, and pretty much everywhere else in this book—and also trips to the most storied Jewish restaurants in the city: Wilensky's Light Lunch, Beauty's Luncheonette, Schwartz's Deli.

Here was a delicatessen culture that was almost exactly like what I'd grown up with in New York, but with some subtle differences. There was salt-cured lox like what I'd get at Russ & Daughters on the Lower East Side, but the bagel it was served on, from a place called St-Viateur, was much smaller than the ones I'd get in New York, with a real hole in the middle and a crisp, fire-burnished skin. At Schwartz's we'd order delicious cured brisket, sold under the name "smoked meat" and served on crusty rye bread, that was much like my beloved New York pastrami, but better—more luscious, smokier, all-around tastier. And of course there was poutine, that Quebecois late-night specialty of gravy-slathered cheese curds atop a bed of French fries. It's not a Jewish thing, per se, but it was an essential part of my Montreal education.

All those foods, the smoked meat especially, became a touchstone of our courtship. When we moved to Brooklyn in 2007—Noah to start law school and I to start a job at the Metropolitan Museum of Art—we brought our shared love of Montreal-style deli with us. What we didn't realize back then was that smoked meat was a food that almost everyone, Montrealers or not, could connect to in a very deep way. And little did we know that if you put it in the bigger context of handmade Jewish deli and home-style dishes, and you elevated those with better ingredients and innovative entrées and good wine and craft beers, something on the order of a runaway chemical reaction would occur. People were longing for this food, even if they didn't know it.

BUT I'M GETTING AHEAD OF MYSELF. By the end of Noah's first year of law school, he knew he wasn't happy, and by the start of the second year, he was looking for anything that could distract him from it. So, in a pique of nostalgia, he started trying to make smoked meat. He got very into making smoked meat. One thing led to another, and, well, things got a little crazy after that. He tells the story better than I can, but the short version is this: By May of 2009 Noah had dropped out of law school. By June we'd signed a lease on a tiny storefront space on Hoyt Street in Boerum Hill. Just after that Noah's Nana Lee died. By October Noah and I were married. By November I'd lost my job at the Met. And then, on January 25, 2010, the restaurant opened, and suddenly I had a new career: running the front of the house at a nineteen-seat Montreal-style Jewish deli while Noah ran the kitchen. We'd decided to call the place Mile End, after the neighborhood in Montreal where his grandparents grew up and where we'd lived together before our journey south. We had ten things on the menu: For the morning service we had a bagel-and-lox plate, a skillet breakfast called the Mish-Mash, and a breakfast sandwich; for the afternoon service we had slaw, pickles, borscht, smoked meat, salami, smoked turkey, and frites and poutine.

I'd never so much as bused a table before, but when we opened, I was the only person taking orders. I simply couldn't believe there were people in this place. And they were lining up to eat our food! At the museum, I'd work for months on an audio guide and rarely get user feedback. But I'd put a sandwich out there and see that smile, see that three-year-old girl lick the plate, and in the same way Noah had always wanted to make something with his hands, I realized that connecting people with our food was my own true calling.

I suppose I should have known that all along. After all, one set of my maternal great-grandparents were chicken farmers—so there's that farm-to-table ethic in my blood—and the others were hoteliers in Lakewood, New Jersey: That's probably where my love of hosting comes from. But the ease with which I fell into this new livelihood had more immediate roots too. When I was growing up, my mother's approach to food was always a bit more gourmet than that of my friends. She was always taking cooking classes, or listening to Arthur Schwartz on the radio and testing new and unusual combinations on me and my more-than-willing friends. But what she really loved was dining out. Whereas Noah's memorable family moments happened around his grandmother's table, ours happened at restaurants of all stripes throughout the city.

I loved when customers would tell me how much this food brought back wonderful and often deep memories for them. They'd tell me stories. About their first pastrami sandwich, about their favorite hometown deli, about some tiny detail they remembered from their grandmother's brisket dinner. I wanted to stick a microphone in their faces. Our cooking meant something to them.

Of course, that upped the pressure on us as well. There's never a matzo ball soup better than your own bubbe's matzo ball soup. We didn't even put chicken soup on the menu for the first four months because we were so afraid of treading on all those grandmotherly legacies. But we'd decided early on that Mile End wasn't going to be a museum of Jewish home cooking or classic deli specialties. You don't have to adhere slavishly to traditional recipes to make great traditional food, just as you don't have to recite the Torah to have a rich spiritual life. We wanted to innovate, improve on the old recipes and the old techniques, use better ingredients, make the food our own.

AND YET, WHAT WE SET OUT to do at Mile End was nothing if not a way for us to connect with our own pasts and families, just like that old shirt Noah was wearing when I first met him was a way for him to stay connected to his grandfather. I think of the two great matriarchs in the Cohen and Bernamoff families, how they're at once fundamentally alike and totally different. Noah's Nana Lee was the ultimate homemaker, while my Grandma Bea was (and still is) a high-powered professional, who graduated from college in the 1940s and to this day is often too busy with her real estate clients to chat when I call her. She made great chicken soup for Shabbos, but nothing like the feasts that Noah's grandmother would assemble on an average Friday night. I think it's really the intersection of these influences that informed our approach to food at Mile End: We wanted to take a cue from Nana's old-world, made-from-scratch ethic and meld it with the forward-thinking ambition of my own grandmother.

At Mile End, and now in this book, we're spreading the gospel of good deli, of bringing good Jewish food into the present tense. This is food for celebration, definitely, but it's also food for a Tuesday night, for every day. It's food for right now. It's food made with love.

—RAE BERNAMOFF

Clockwise, from top: Rae's great-grandparents,
Spruce Street Farm, Lakewood, New Jersey,
late 1940s; Hotel Lieberman, New Year's Eve,
1949; Spruce Street Farm chicken coop

DEAR NEIGHBORS, FRIENDS, CURIOUS ONLOOKERS, DELIPHILES, CRAZED NOSTALGISTS, SYMPATHETIC VEGETARIANS, SELF-HATING JEWS, CANADIENS FANS, LUMBERJACKS, CHILDREN OF THE MULROUNY ERA, AND LOVERS OF ALL THINGS "MONTREALAISE" MILE END WILL FINALLY OPEN FOR BREAKFAST, LUNCH, AND DINNER THIS MONDAY, JANUARY 25, 2010. THANKS FOR THE ENTHUSIASM AND PATIENCE.
NOAH & RAE

Clockwise, from top left: Mile End Delicatessen; signage from our 2010 opening; slicing brisket

Introduction

OUR STORY OPENS ON THE ROOF of a four-story walk-up in Park Slope, Brooklyn. The characters are me, Rae, an eighteen-inch Weber Bullet smoker, and many pounds of expensive, beautifully marbled beef brisket. Oh, those poor, sacrificial briskets. I had no idea what I was doing. I didn't have the correct tools, I wasn't using the right kind of wood, I didn't even have curing salt. I was impatient, too: I didn't let the meat cure long enough, or I'd make the fire too hot, or I'd get distracted and let it go out. Most of those carbonized, oversalted briskets went into the garbage. Rae suffered through the rest.

So began my quest to make smoked meat, the most sacred of Montreal delicatessen foods. It started out as homesickness, a longing for familiar flavors that New York's pastrami and corned beef couldn't quite replicate, but soon it became my holy grail. And, though I didn't know it at the time, my attempts to make smoked meat were merely the first leg of an all-consuming journey into the world of do-it-yourself delicatessen and Jewish home cooking. That journey culminated in Mile End, the restaurant that Rae and I opened on Hoyt Street in Brooklyn in January 2010, less than two years after my first battles with brisket on our Park Slope rooftop.

To call it a whirlwind journey doesn't quite capture the about-face I made in those two years. I was supposed to be a lawyer. My cousins were doctors and lawyers, and I knew I would make my Nana happy. It's what I'd come to New York City from Montreal to do. At first I embraced the intense study, but I quickly discovered that writing briefs and cloistering myself in the library at Brooklyn Law School were not playing to my strengths. I longed to work with my hands, to get out into the city, to be a part of the life of Brooklyn. I pined for my Montreal days—McGill, playing bass in my old band, The Lovely Feathers, and the overall energy of the city. I missed eating the Wilensky Special, the gravy-drenched poutine at Patati Patata, and the smoked meat sandwiches and full-sour pickles at Schwartz's Deli. Law school was a sensory wasteland for me. Unable to immerse myself in it, I sought refuge in brisket and wood smoke.

Admittedly, I didn't have much to work with. I trolled bookstores and the Web for smoked meat recipes and came up empty-handed. I found excellent recipes for making corned beef and plenty of effusive blog posts about the quality of Montreal's smoked meat, but aside from a few threads about pastrami, nothing was useful. What I soon realized is that even among die-hard carnivores, smoked meat isn't something people try to do at home. To make matters worse, virtually no one outside of Canada had even heard of it. The tips about smoking brisket that I did find weren't coming from Jewish cooks or deli men but from the world of southern barbecue. In spirit, if not in method, I took inspiration from these pit-masters; I admired their determination to master an age-old, folklore-drenched cooking style in their own backyards.

I started by cobbling together a list of spices, herbs, and everything else anyone had ever used to make pastrami and corned beef and went from there. I began experimenting with the basic ratios of salt to sugar, and decided that if I could get the science right, then everything else would be left to my taste and sense of nostalgia.

Eventually I learned how to manage the smoker— how to keep it going strong for eight hours—maybe not at the exact right temperature at first, but I soon sorted that out, too. I learned to be patient and not disturb the brisket as it sat in the fridge covered in its curing rub. Then I made the crucial discovery that plunging the meat into fresh water before smoking tempered the excessive saltiness that had been plaguing my briskets. That was a turning point. Suddenly, everything clicked. The brisket came out of the smoker tender and flavorful, the meat fatty and redolent of garlic and coriander. This was smoked meat the way I remembered it! It was different from Schwartz's—the benchmark—but it was good, and most important, it was mine.

Soon I was smoking whole turkeys up on that roof. Shortly thereafter I began making my own pickles. Then I was salt-curing salmon for lox, grinding beef to make my own salami, roasting chicken skin to render my own schmaltz. Law school became a distraction from cooking, instead of the other way around.

A combination of a few occurences ultimately pushed me in the right direction: I noticed an absurdly inexpensive, miniature storefront available for rent on Hoyt Street along my bike route to and from law school; I went through an arduous exam period at a time when the American economy was imploding and law students, in particular, experienced a catastrophic decrease in employment opportunities—and I had a series of conversations with six people who I knew loved me without qualification: Rae; my parents, Brenda and Kenny; Rae's parents, Jeryl and Itzhak; and my close friend Max Levine. When the concept for Mile End was first discussed, it wasn't much more than scrawls on the back of a napkin, yet somehow, the whole gang supported the project. I haphazardly signed a lease.

I wish running a restaurant were pure pleasure; in reality, it's pleasure adulterated by difficult decisions, exhaustion, and the constant ebb and flow of emotion. Staying on top of everything that needed to happen with the business, cooking for sixteen hours a day, and managing the staff were quite a challenge that first year. To help ease the burden, we welcomed Max as a co-manager of the business in January of 2011. Max continually helps me think through tough situations, often unrelated to business, and is one of the few people capable of keeping me in check, especially when my temper flares—he has a remarkable ability to remain patient and calm in stressful situations. Without his sacrifice and voice of reason, Rae and I would still be struggling to understand the mechanisms of supply and demand. Mile End would still be a little deli on Hoyt.

IF I HAD TO PICK A SINGLE FOOD or ingredient that embodies what we do at Mile End today, it wouldn't in fact be the smoked meat sandwich, even though that remains our most popular and talked-about menu item. It'd have to be the schmaltz. We make our own schmaltz every day, and we use it for everything—as a seasoning, as a cooking fat, even to enrich our baked goods. We use it instead of oil in our vinaigrette. What's not to like about schmaltz? It's a pure, unprocessed fat, made naturally from chicken skin that might otherwise go to waste. It's rich and flavorful, and it's easy to make more when you run out. Plus, the chicken skin cracklings that are left over on the roasting tray once the schmaltz has rendered make an insanely delicious little accoutrement called gribenes that was once as beloved among Jewish cooks as schmaltz itself. For me, schmaltz is the symbol par excellence of the age-old

resourcefulness of Jewish cooks, who were doing nose-to-tail cuisine centuries before it became a hip urban trend. Nothing wasted, everything savored.

In my mind, schmaltz embodied the from-scratch philosophy we had in mind when we were planning the menu for our deli. It was, and still is, a sort of talisman for me. But the truth is, schmaltz wasn't part of the Mile End repertoire at first. I was thinking less about old-fashioned Ashkenazi home cooking than I was about Montreal delis and casse-croutes. Originally I envisioned Mile End as little more than a poutine-and-smoked-meat joint that served wine and beer. Maybe we'd serve brunch too: Montreal-style bagels, say, with a schmear and some lox. Basically a Montreal greatest-hits album.

Then my Nana Lee died a few months before we planned to open. This woman was the glue that held my family together. And the reason my family happily allowed themselves to be glued was Nana Lee's food. Her food, and her huge Friday-night dinners, gave structure and substance to our lives. My memories of her meals, more than my memories of Schwartz's or any other deli, were what really fueled my love of eating and cooking. Maybe I overreacted, but when she died I thought to myself: Is this the end? Will this food find someplace to live on in our lives?

Suddenly everything shifted into focus. This restaurant we were about to open had to be a Jewish restaurant. There would be the deli classics, sure, and maybe bagels with homemade lox, but there'd be borscht too. There'd be a Wilensky. There'd be smoked turkey. There'd be mandelbrot and cheese bagelach and honey cake. There would be schmaltz.

Of course, we did not achieve this right off the bat. Before we could accomplish much of anything, we had to solve a rather towering problem of supply and demand. We got an inkling of the struggle ahead a couple of months before we even opened, when an article about us appeared in *New York* magazine. It was written by the preeminent deli historian—and now our good friend—David Sax, and it contained a huge, close-up color photo of a smoked meat sandwich I'd made. It was a very good photograph. Local food blogs picked up the story, and within days, people were showing up on Hoyt Street clutching the article, peering in through the

For me, schmaltz is the symbol par excellence of the age-old resourcefulness of Jewish cooks, who were doing nose-to-tail cuisine centuries before it became a hip urban trend. Nothing wasted, everything savored.

....

newspaper-covered windows, asking if they could get a smoked meat sandwich. By the time we actually opened, in January, it was chaos.

Mile End is a small place; even by New York standards, 430 square feet is not much—just four tables and five counter stools, plus a street-side takeout window. The kitchen is a narrow galley with a few shelves for storage in the back. We had one little smoker, which was working all the time, even overnight, and we were still selling out of smoked meat by lunchtime, at which point we simply had to close. I felt like we'd created a monster.

Slowly but surely, things got better. The following June we rented a modest warehouse a few blocks from the deli, a place large enough to build a basic kitchen that could handle our supply problem. The kitchen gave us another luxury: prep space.

We hired real cooks and a baker, a few of whom came to us unbidden based on what they'd heard about the place or experienced as customers. James Merker, Sam Filloramo, Rich Maggi, Michael Stokes—these were brilliant guys with restaurant chops who understood our vision. I remember Michael just showing up one day with his own homemade rye bread and a box of little homemade jams and sauces and cheeses. Holy shit, I thought, who is this guy? We hired him on the spot. Still one of the best decisions I have made since Mile End

opened. Michael is officially our director of operations, managing the daily challenges of food production from the warehouse kitchen. Unofficially, he is the elder statesman of the company, ever-patient, leading by example. A more committed employee there is not; Michael's mastery of the kitchen is evident in the food at the deli and the recipes in this book.

Before long, in place of a menu of Montreal deli staples that changed little from breakfast through dinner, we had something resembling a proper restaurant menu. Some of our new items were orthodox renditions of Jewish classics, but most of our entrées were not. We were developing innovative, ingredient-driven dishes that related to Jewish tradition in a way that reflected the type of food we wanted to eat. We had a tongue sandwich, that most old-school of deli offerings, made not with sliced beef tongue, but with dainty pickled lamb's tongues split lengthwise, griddled, and served with pumpernickel toasts and a red wine–onion marmalade. I liked the subtle flavor of lamb's tongue. We had a fish entrée, but it wasn't a smoked-salmon platter; it was pan-seared trout served with our house-made salt shallots, horseradish cream, and pickled beets. I knew of a great freshwater fishery just a hundred miles north of the city, and so why not serve local trout? We picked interesting small-production wines to go with the dishes, and we expanded our selection of craft beers.

Everything, right down to the condiments, was made from scratch, from the pickled tomatoes and preserved lemons served with our veal schnitzel to the cheese filling and compote served with our blintzes. We made a daily batch of schmaltz, which we'd spread on slices of our fresh-baked challah before toasting and topping it with our chicken salad (which in turn was made with our own lemon mayonnaise and topped with our own gribenes). Heaven.

This wasn't purebred Jewish deli or even Montreal deli, and it wasn't textbook Jewish home-cooked comfort food, either. Nor was it strictly kosher. It was a reflection of our own eating experiences. I grew up eating bacon and eggs on Sunday mornings with my dad—and, not infrequently, Chinese roast pork for dinner—so we put bacon on our breakfast sandwich and served delicious homemade Chinese food on Christmas.

It was liberating. The traditional boundaries of Jewish food fell away. I'd proved to myself that you can make deli food at home, and at Mile End we proved that you can have great Jewish home cooking at a restaurant—and it doesn't have to be on a holiday or according to strict dietary regulations.

Erasing those boundaries did not come without consequences. We heard: This isn't real deli, or real Jewish food, or real Montreal food. People had strong feelings about delis, and we'd clearly strayed into some very sensitive territory.

Rae and I found ourselves asking, What is authentic Jewish food, anyhow? For many Jews of my parents' generation it was powdered soup mix and Manischewitz. And yes, the taste of those things may be just as sacred to them as schmaltz and gribenes were to their Eastern European forebears, or good smoked meat is to me. For Rae and me, *authentic* means making everything ourselves; it means offering the kind of food we'd want to serve in our own home. It means breathing new life into traditional techniques like pickling, curing, and smoking. It means nurturing a respect for very good ingredients, knowing where they come from, making friends with our butcher and fishmonger and farmer. It means knowing what's in season and what's not. And the beautiful part is, none of this is new to Jewish cooking; this is the way our ancestors did it for generations. It's just that these practices got lost over the years, through migration and exile and assimilation.

This book is our attempt to bring the best elements of the cuisine back into the everyday American vocabulary—and to improve on them. The recipes are almost entirely faithful to what we do at Mile End, just scaled down for the home kitchen. We don't have any secret formulas that can't be replicated.

We want to make deli food a vital part of the American landscape again. And we want real Jewish comfort food to be as much a part of everyday American life as Italian food is. Both have honest peasant roots, both are only as good as the raw ingredients they're made from, and both have a nearly infinite capacity to provide comfort and express love. This is a book you can pick up any day of the week and cook from. Once you start making your own pickled asparagus and your own rugelach and your own lamb sausage, it opens up a whole new dimension in your cooking. It awakens that desire to experiment, to innovate, all while getting back in touch with older, better ways of cooking and thinking about food. Without tradition you'll never be able to innovate, and without innovation you'll never really be able to revive your traditions.

NOT LONG AFTER MY NANA LEE DIED, my parents were sorting through her belongings and came across a small box containing a handful of handwritten recipes and even more new, blank index cards. It turns out my grandmother had started the process of writing down the family recipes, but hadn't had time to finish the project. What had compelled her after all these years?

A while later, after Rae and I had opened Mile End, my sister told me she had a theory. She said she thought that Nana Lee somehow knew about my decision to leave law school, despite my parents' assurances that they'd kept it a secret. Not only that, but my sister also believed that our grandmother knew I was going to become a cook and a restaurateur and that maybe, just maybe, she was writing down those recipes for me.

It's a humbling notion, the truth never to be known. In the end I suppose it doesn't matter. What my grandmother didn't have time to teach me in substance she gave me a thousandfold in spirit, in love, and in food. Now I'm just passing it all on.

—NOAH BERNAMOFF

Counterclockwise, from top left: Nana Lee
and Grandpa Sid on the balcony of their Parc
Avenue apartment, 1940s; Noah's mother,
grandmother and aunts in the kitchen, 1982

How to Use This Book

THIS BOOK IS ALL ABOUT overturning the assumptions that have long governed Jewish food—namely, that deli specialties like smoked meat and lox are things you never make at home, and that the Jewish food you do make at home is just matzo ball soup, latkes, and other bubbe classics reserved for the holidays.

Part 1, the "Do-It-Yourself Delicatessen," is where you'll find recipes that teach you how to make delicatessen classics at home. This section has two chapters: one for meat and fish preparations (think salami, smoked turkey, gefilte fish), and another for pickles, condiments, fillings, and garnishes (think sour cucumbers, horseradish cream, gribenes).

These DIY preparations, in essence, are the building blocks for the second section of the book, "To the Table," which contains recipes for finished dishes. DIY preparations are conveniently cross-referenced in the ingredient list of each finished-dish recipe. Though the joy that comes from eating a sandwich for which you made the bread, meat, and condiments from scratch is nearly unmatched, it is a time-consuming endeavor that requires long-lead planning. Don't despair if you haven't got time to whip up every element of the meal: These recipes will still turn out great with good-quality, store-bought versions of the same ingredients, many of which are also available at mileenddeli.com to help you get started.

The book is also peppered with wisdom from friends in Brooklyn and beyond whom we consider to be geniuses in their field. These pieces include tips on buying and caring for your knives, advice on choosing meat and poultry, a short history of Jewish appetizing, and a lot more. You'll also find an equipment primer (at right), some helpful notes on ingredients (page 22), step-by-step instructions for slicing brisket (page 23), and a selection of holiday menus (page 212).

Equipment

MILE END'S FOOD IS COMFORT FOOD, plain and simple. That doesn't mean it's unsophisticated, or that everything we do is as easy as mac and cheese. It just means that the dishes and preparations in this book are meant to bring you pleasure again and again. That's why it's worth it to have the right equipment. Fortunately, you probably already own most of the gear you'll need, and if you don't, the tools these recipes call for are not wildly expensive or hard to find. (Check out our Resources section on page 216 for specific information on where to buy.) While it's safe to say that our forebearers in the shtetls of Eastern and Central Europe didn't have electric stand mixers or digital meat thermometers, they almost certainly had sturdy stockpots, well-cared-for butcher blocks, and decent knives. This is pretty basic stuff. What's more, these tools will be lifelong companions in the kitchen, no matter what kind of cuisine you're making.

SMOKER, GAS GRILL, OR CHARCOAL KETTLE GRILL
Smoking is a cornerstone of our cooking at Mile End, and if you plan to do a lot of smoking at home like we do, you might want to buy a dedicated smoker. We like the charcoal-burning Smokey Mountain Cookers made by Weber—often called "bullet" smokers because of their shape—which are essentially elongated kettle grills with two grilling grates that keep the food well away from the coals to facilitate slow, low indirect-heat cooking. Basic models can be had for a few hundred dollars, and there is a wide selection available on the Internet.

That said, you can execute the smoked meat, smoked turkey, and other smoked preparations in this book splendidly with a standard gas or charcoal grill. It's all in the setup and in the patient, careful tending of the fire and smoke.

But first, the wood, which is where all that smoky flavor comes from. You'll want to find good-quality hardwood chips. We keep a variety in our larder for different preparations: tannic, assertive woods such as hickory, and lighter fruit woods like apple and cherry, as well as neutral, consistent woods like oak. We recommend using oak as a base with a little added hickory for smoked meat, and apple or cherry for poultry and fish. Nonetheless, oak independently does a great job across the board. Wood chips are often sold in five-pound bags; this is a good starting quantity to have on hand. The amount of chips per recipe will be dependent on the duration of the smoke, the size of your smoker, and the outdoor temperature. You can buy a fancy firebox for the chips, but you can also simply fashion a pouch out of two layers of aluminum foil and poke holes in it with a fork. That pouch can go directly onto the fire. Be sure to soak the wood chips in cold water for a half hour or so before cooking.

Because of their constant fuel source, gas grills are the easier option. You're going to need one with at least two separate burners with separate controls and, ideally, at least two removable grill grates. (The pretty basic Weber gas model we have at home has all these things.) Remove one of the grill grates and put your wood-chip pouch as close to the outermost burner as possible. (Many grills have protective sheaths over the burner vents; the pouch can go right on top of those.) Turn on that burner and set it to medium heat to get those wood chips going; then lower the heat. Leave the other burners off and set your meat or poultry or fish on the grill grate over the inactive burners. Then shut the lid and let that smoke and indirect heat do the work.

If you're smoking a big piece of meat—like, say, a fifteen-pound brisket for the Smoked Meat recipe on page 33—you can count on having to replace the wood chips with a new pouch at least twice during the course of cooking. So make sure you have presoaked chips at the ready. And remember that you'll need to raise the heat of the active burner to get the new chips going before lowering it again.

If you're using a charcoal grill, mass the coals on one side and place the wood-chip pouch directly onto them, keeping the food as far away from the coals as possible. (You can also put the wood directly onto the coals, with no foil pouch, but if you choose this method, use soaked wood chunks instead of chips, and count on having to add a lot more wood during

cooking than you would using a pouch.) As with a gas grill, you'll have to swap in a new wood-chip pouch after a couple of hours. Unlike a gas grill, the charcoal grill will also need refueling. Hardwood lump charcoal (the kind we recommend) burns hot for only an hour or so, meaning you'll have to do multiple small re-ups of charcoal during the cooking of a big piece of meat or poultry. Keep in mind that removing the food while adding charcoal or wood chips causes it to cool down, making for a longer cooking time (and making a good meat thermometer so essential). We recommend consulting the instructions that were included with your smoker or grill; they will provide guidelines for the particularities of your equipment.

MEAT THERMOMETER
Of all the supposedly time-saving digital gadgets, few have made our lives easier than the digital probe meat thermometer. If you like to smoke meat, this tool is a godsend. You just stick the probe into the thickest part of the meat and then leave the end of the probe cord dangling outside of the grill or smoker. Whenever you want to check the food's internal temperature, just plug the cord into the digital reader. No need to open the smoker's lid and release all that precious smoke.

DIGITAL INSTANT-READ THERMOMETER
This is useful for a variety of tasks. Try to find one that has a temperature range up to 400°F. You can use it for just about anything, including frying, baking, or testing meat. (Just don't leave it in the meat while smoking or roasting, because the LED display can be damaged by high heat.)

STAND MIXER
If you're going to buy one big-ticket item for your kitchen, let it be a KitchenAid stand mixer. For the kind of from-scratch cooking that this book calls for, the KitchenAid mixer, with its multiple attachments, strong motor, and sturdy housing, is a huge time-saver. If baking is your thing, the stand mixer will be your greatest ally. Knishes (page 165), Hamantaschen (page 201), Apple Turnovers (page 111), Challah (page 177),

Pletzel (page 184)—almost all the fabulous baked goods in the Jewish canon are so much easier to make, and make well, with this appliance.

If you're going to splurge on a stand mixer, we recommend also springing for the meat-grinder attachment, which is good for making a number of the meat-based dishes in this book.

MEAT GRINDER AND SAUSAGE STUFFER

Many kitchens have a food processor, and it might be tempting to use it in place of a meat grinder when a recipe calls for one of those. But if you use a processor, chances are that you're going to end up with pulverized meat, not ground meat. So either buy the meat-grinder attachment for your stand mixer (see above) or pick up a simple, easy-to-clean hand-cranked meat grinder. Ideally, you'll want one that can be fitted with both a coarse grinding plate and a fine one, as some of the recipes in this book call for grinding the meat coarsely as a first step, to facilitate the mixing-in of spices and flavorings, and then passing a portion of that coarsely ground meat through a fine plate to achieve a more variegated texture.

If you're going to make your own salami (page 36) or other homemade cased meats, get your hands on a sausage stuffer. Unfortunately, the stuffing attachment on the KitchenAid stand mixer tends to emulsify the meat, thus destroying the coarse texture and appearance essential to a good salami. Instead, choose a hand-cranked meat grinder that also has a stuffing tube attachment. Or, for a little more money, you can get yourself a dedicated hand-cranked sausage stuffer, which is basically a piston that pushes the meat through a tube. You can spend more than that on high-end stainless steel models, but there's no need to. Hardened-aluminum versions work just fine. Just be sure to clean your stuffer really well after each use, and let it dry completely after washing. Sausagemaker .com is a great source for stuffers and grinders—and all things cased meat–related.

PASTA ROLLER

We cherish this tool. And not just for making pasta. It's perfect for rolling out Knishes (page 165) and for making Matzo (page 187). For us the sine qua non of pasta rollers is the Atlas: durable, reliable, and easy to use.

FOOD MILL

We make a lot of applesauce in the fall and winter, and to do it right, you need a hand-cranked food mill.

FOOD PROCESSOR

We don't recommend it for grinding meat (see above), but it sure is wonderful for just about everything else. At home we use our food processor to shred cabbage for Coleslaw (page 133) and Sauerkraut (page 82), to chop big amounts of garlic if we're making a rub for smoked meat or a spice mix for salami, and for so many other tasks. Just make sure you buy a processor that comes with both chopping blades and a grating disk. Cuisinart and Waring are both good choices.

STEAK WEIGHT

If you've ever been to a diner, you've probably seen the line cook using one of these. It's an almost brutishly simple thing: a heavy rectangle of metal with a handle attached. We'd never use it on a steak, but it's essential for making our griddled, pressed Ruth Wilensky sandwich (page 122), and it is the key, in our opinion, to the perfect grilled cheese.

SPICE GRINDER OR COFFEE MILL

We always recommend grinding whole spices yourself. You can do it by hand with a mortar and pestle, but you're going to have tired wrists after making some of the recipes in this book. An electric coffee-bean grinder dedicated to spice grinding will work just fine— you can get one inexpensively.

FOOD-GRADE PLASTIC CONTAINERS

Flip to almost any page in this book and you'll probably see the word *brining*, *pickling*, or *curing*. These age-old methods of food preservation and flavoring are a foundation of what we do at Mile End, so it's absolutely essential that we have plenty of food-safe, nonreactive vessels to work with. Don't use an aluminum or copper vessel for these preparations, because the acids in the pickling or curing solutions will react with the metal and impart nasty flavors to the food. Stainless steel is considered the ultimate nonreactive kitchen material, but you don't need heavy steel for brining a turkey in the fridge or for letting a brisket sit in its curing rub. For these we recommend big, cheap, food-grade plastic containers—you can buy them at almost any kitchen-supply or housewares store—and big plastic turkey-brining bags (also widely available). We use comparatively expensive Lexan containers at Mile End, but you won't need anything that fancy. Ceramic and glass work well, and in fact, for many of our pickling, curing, and brining preparations you can get by with nothing more than a brining bag set on a rimmed baking sheet.

LARGE NONREACTIVE STOCKPOT

Many of the brining solutions called for in our pickling and curing recipes need to be boiled before use, and for that you're going to need a big pot—at least ten to twelve quarts and, ideally, stainless steel, which won't react with the acids in those solutions. Again, stay away from copper and aluminum.

KNIVES

It's hard to overstate the value of a set of sharp, good-quality knives. At home we basically rely on three: an eight- or ten-inch chef's knife, which does the bulk of the work around our kitchen; a serrated knife for slicing bread; and a five- to five-and-a-half-inch blade known as a paring knife, which is great for both peeling and precision cutting. Turn to page 43 to learn some tips from our friend Joel Bukiewicz, an artisan knife-maker in Brooklyn, on choosing and caring for your knives—and on finding the right sharpening tool.

WOOD BUTCHER BLOCK

For us, a heavy slab of wood (we like the long-grain butcher blocks made near the deli by Brooklyn Butcher Blocks) is still the ultimate cutting surface. It's gentle on knives and beautiful to look at. The trick is in the maintenance. Keep your butcher block clean and dry, washing it with soap and water after every use and drying it by hand. And periodically treat it with food-safe mineral oil to keep the wood from drying out, fraying, and cracking. Steer clear of boards that have a finish or veneer, which can break down over time. If the surface of your board starts to deteriorate, or if the grooves get too deep, you can sand and oil the surface.

Ingredients

ALMOST ALL OF THE ingredients you'll need for making the recipes in this book are widely available at good supermarkets, butcher shops, and other neighborhood purveyors. A few exceptions are cited below (see Resources on page 216 for buying information), as are helpful notes on staple ingredients that appear repeatedly in the recipes.

SALT AND PEPPER

Unless otherwise specified, "salt" in a recipe means kosher salt—specifically, Diamond Crystal kosher salt, which is the brand we recommend. This is important because different brands of salt are produced differently. Diamond Crystal salt is produced by pan evaporation, which creates semi-hollow pyramid-shaped crystals. Morton salt is produced by rolling the salt between rollers to create flat flakes of salt. The result is that a tablespoon of Morton actually contains nearly twice as much salt as a tablespoon of Diamond Crystal. The difference when using table salt or fine sea salt is even greater. A tablespoon of table salt is equal to 2¼ tablespoons of Diamond Crystal. Use half a teaspoon of Morton kosher salt or table salt for every teaspoon of Diamond Crystal. *Never* use iodized salt for these recipes (especially the meat and pickle recipes), because the iodine can change the results.

When we say "black pepper," we always mean the freshly ground kind, milled on the spot from whole peppercorns, not the preground stuff that comes in a shaker. Standard Tellicherry black peppercorns are just fine.

PINK CURING SALT

This curing salt—sometimes sold under the name Instacure No. 1 or Prague Powder #1—is essential for making salami and other cased meats. It's basically table salt mixed with food coloring and a little sodium nitrate, a compound that inhibits the growth of food-borne bacteria.

SAUSAGE CASINGS

A heavy cased meat like salami calls for a relatively sturdy synthetic casing that can withstand the pressure of stuffing and the expansion that happens when the meat is smoked. We use synthetic collagen casings for our beef salami at Mile End. Sausagemaker.com sells them in a variety of sizes. Be sure to follow the product instructions for soaking and flushing the casings before use (this makes them more malleable).

For our breakfast sausages and other smaller cased meats, we use natural sheep casings, which usually come prewashed and packed in a saltwater solution that needs to be rinsed off before use.

BUTTER

Anytime you see "butter" in one of our recipes, we mean the unsalted kind.

SUGAR

"Sugar" means plain old white granulated sugar, unless otherwise noted.

HERBS

All herbs called for in the recipes are fresh herbs—even bay leaves—except in some of the curing recipes, where we specifically call for dried herbs.

FLOUR AND COARSE DECORATIVE SUGAR

We get most of our flour and all of our decorative sugar from King Arthur Flour.

CHOCOLATE

"Chocolate" means bittersweet chocolate. Valrhona, Ghirardelli, and Baker's are widely available brands.

How to Slice Smoked Meat

PROPER MONTREAL-STYLE SMOKED MEAT, in our opinion, has to be made from a whole brisket. This will comprise both the flat (also called the first cut, which is typically all you get when you buy a brisket at the supermarket) and the fattier, underappreciated deckle (sometimes called the point). In a whole brisket, the flat and the deckle are separated by a membrane of fat that runs at a shallow diagonal through the cut, creating two tapered lobes. A smoked meat sandwich without at least a couple of slices of that luxuriously fatty deckle isn't really a smoked meat sandwich, as far as we're concerned. The trick in slicing a whole smoked brisket is in managing the cut's uneven shape and its changing grain in order to end up with fairly uniform slices that aren't overcooked. Here's how to do it:

1 After steaming the brisket following the instructions in the recipe on page 35, start by slicing the smaller, tapered portion of the flat (which will already have been separated from the thicker part of the brisket, because it steams faster). Determine the direction of the meat's grain by looking at the underside, which is not obscured by the fat cap. Then simply start slicing at ninety degrees against the grain. Well, *simply* is a relative term: Since you're not dealing with a perfectly rectangular cut of meat, you may need to cheat the angle a bit toward the tapered end so that you don't end up with sad little medallions in lieu of broad slices. But don't worry if every slice isn't the same length; just try to avoid super-small pieces, which are the enemy of a well-built sandwich.

2 Arguably more important than the length of each is its thickness. And a good sandwich has uniform slices. We typically go for a quarter-inch or thinner. Here's where a long-tined carving fork comes in very handy. It will not only stabilize the meat while you're cutting, but also serve as your thickness guide. Orienting the fork so that the curve of the tines faces inward, pierce the meat at roughly one-inch intervals, and then make four quarter-inch slices at a time, working your knife toward the fork until, with the last of the four cuts, the face of the blade actually brushes up gently against the tines. Then move your fork outward another inch and repeat.

3 When the bigger, back section of the brisket is done steaming, pull it out and lay it on your cutting board. Now it's time to separate the deckle from the remaining portion of the flat—an essential step, because the two sections do not have parallel grains. To do this, locate the membrane of fat separating the flat from the deckle; it should be visible where you made the initial cut before steaming. Then start slicing inward along the path of that fat membrane until you've cut clear through to the other side. When you're done, trim away and discard that ribbon of fat from both sections of meat—don't worry, it's not the delicious kind of fat!

4 Now you can start slicing these two sections following the instructions in steps 2 and 3. With one additional caveat: Since these portions of meat are quite large, they can yield unmanageably long slices as you work your way toward the wide midsection of the cuts. Thus, when you get to that midsection, you may want to halve the meat along the grain and slice the two halves separately.

5 Finally, it's time to build your sandwich. See page 121 for the recipe.

A Jewish Deli, Born Again

BY DAVID SAX, AUTHOR OF *SAVE THE DELI*

"HEY, DAVID," Noah Bernamoff wrote to me in our first-ever correspondence, back in August 2009. "I thought I should send a cordial greeting your way. Indeed the Jewish deli is a dying breed, and its loss is not limited to our culinary traditions but to the recognition of our Eastern European roots and ultimately our historical sense of place and culture, or Yiddishkeit. As someone who was raised on my bubbe's pickled herring, chopped liver, matzo ball soup, and mandelbrot, I feel the same urgency as you; as that generation slowly passes away, we are left with a Jewish demographic unwilling to carry on the beautiful traditions of the past."

Noah went on to describe Mile End, the deli that he and his fiancée, Rae Cohen, were planning to open in Brooklyn. He was hardly the first aspiring deli man I'd talked to. Since launching the blog Savethedeli.com in early 2007—a precursor to a book by the same name that I published two years later—I'd heard from plenty of concerned deli lovers and entrepreneurs. Mostly they said the same things: They grew up eating deli, there was no great deli where they lived, they wanted to bring great deli back. Some of these people went on to open delicatessens, and a few were successful.

Noah had never run a business, never worked in a restaurant, and never really cooked outside of his own home. But something stood out in his e-mail that hinted at greater ambitions. "My hope," he wrote, "is that Mile End will not only highlight the foods (Montreal smoked meat, kosher-style salami, smoked fish, pickled veggies, everything homemade using organic and free-range ingredients) but embody the indelible warmth and love associated with the food and the tradition."

This guy had passion and chutzpah, and a refreshingly simple idea: creating classic Jewish deli using the do-it-yourself, nose-to-tail methods that had become the calling card of young urban chefs in recent years. It'd be tempting to say that this was revolutionary. It wasn't. In fact, it was devolutionary. Really, what Noah was proposing was a return to the fold for Yiddish cooking, which had strayed far from its made-from-scratch roots, nearly taking the deli down with it. After more than a

century in existence, as Noah had pointed out in his e-mail—and as I'd been preaching to anyone who would listen—the Jewish delicatessen was in a state of malaise.

THE FOODS AT THE CORE of the present-day delicatessen came from Eastern European Jewish home kitchens, which adapted Polish, Russian, Hungarian, and other regional dishes into kosher variations, tweaked those, and made them central to life in Jewish Europe for much of the past millennium. These included preserved meats, like duck sausage and smoked turkey; fish, like pickled herring, lox, and the slippery gefilte; pickled vegetables; and a bevy of hearty mains and sides starting with the letter *K* (kreplach, knishes, kugel, kasha). These were simple, fortifying, delicious peasant foods.

The modern deli grew from those traditions and is, essentially, a creature of exile. It started its life in the late nineteenth century, in the dense immigrant slums of cities like New York, Chicago, London, Paris, and Montreal, where poor, newly arrived Yiddish-speaking Jews—many driven from Russia and Eastern Europe by the terror of the tsar—lived and worked. Kosher butchers, who often slaughtered their animals in the street, began opening lunch counters that sold cured or preserved meats, such as corned beef, pickled tongue, baked salamis, and smoked pastrami, as a way of creating value-added products from excess inventory. Over time, these simple kosher takeout shops—many of which began to call themselves delicatessens, from the French for delicacies, or delicious things to eat—got the idea to place their meats between slices of bread, following a growing food trend in North America. These inner-city delis thrived, and with success came permanent seating, waiter service, and an expanded menu that included hot dishes. The kosher delicatessen soon became the Jewish version of the American diner.

By the start of the Second World War, the Jewish deli was a recognized cultural institution in North American cities, among Jews and non-Jews alike. Pastrami and corned beef had become part of the dining lexicon, and people went out for deli the way folks go out for Italian food today. Deli was an accepted and warmly embraced ethnic diversion. By the 1930s, there were between three and four thousand Jewish delis in New York City alone. Eager to gain a wider audience, many Jewish delis assimilated, dropping the pretense of being kosher, letting more traditional foods like gribenes and schmaltz fall by the wayside, and even putting spaghetti and lobster on the menu.

After World War II, with Eastern Europe's and Russia's Jewish population decimated, Jewish immigration slowed to a trickle, cutting off the source of both customers and proprietors for future delis. The deli faced other obstacles as well. Starting in the 1950s, suburbanization began to break up the tight-knit immigrant communities where small delis could thrive, replacing the inner-city mom-and-pop model with shopping plazas and huge, full-service suburban restaurants. What's more, the rise of suburban supermarkets cut deeply into delis' takeout business. Instead of buying bread, soup mandel, egg noodles, horseradish cream, and roast beef from the local deli or kosher bakery, Jewish housewives could now gather all these items into one basket at their local grocery store, which now sold shelf-stable powdered and canned kosher products made by companies like Manischewitz and Streit's.

Owing to the absence of fresh immigrants from the old world and the pressures of assimilation, the flavors of the Yiddish motherland became an increasingly distant memory, pushed aside by hamburgers, Chinese food, and Rice-A-Roni. Jewish old-world cooking, that pillar of everyday life for so many generations of Ashkenazi families, was now trotted out only on special occasions and holidays, the scoop of chopped liver taking on an almost religious significance at the Passover table. The recipes, the cooking skills, and the sense-memory of those foods were not being passed on to new generations. Those aging grandparents with mustard in their veins—like Noah's Nana Lee—watched powerless as their grandchildren eschewed blintzes for California rolls.

Meanwhile, delis were disappearing by the hundreds. In many places where they'd previously thrived, like Kansas City or Miami Beach, they would soon disappear completely, while in New York City, the deli heartland itself, thousands became just a few

dozen. Many of those that did hang on had lost their bearings. As their customers disappeared and their kosher suppliers dwindled, many deli owners were forced to outsource much of their food production. Meats, once cured and smoked in-house, were bought in bulk from industrial producers and then steamed to order at the deli. Sauerkraut came out of a can, coleslaw and pickles from a tub. The result was that the food from one Jewish deli to the next started to taste exactly the same—the same Hebrew National pastrami, the same Pechter's rye, the same Gulden's mustard. Many delis became nostalgia acts, just churning out the greatest hits, like the Steve Miller Band of matzo ball soup and corned beef sandwiches. Reduced to survival mode, the Jewish delicatessen had stopped evolving.

AND YET ALL WAS NOT LOST. Even before Mile End opened, change was in the air. Starting in the mid-2000s, I'd witnessed the rise of several notable exceptions to the sad norm. In Portland, Oregon, Ken Gordon and Nick Zukin had turned a home-smoked pastrami experiment at a farmers' market into a thriving restaurant called Kenny and Zuke's, which made its own meats, bread, bagels, lox, knishes, bialys, and other delicacies and served them to a hip crowd in the Ace Hotel. In Toronto, a young home cook named Zane Caplan started making smoked meat in his backyard, eventually moved the operation into the abandoned kitchen of a tavern, and parlayed his success into Caplansky's, a delicatessen that boasted freshly made kishke and house-made lox and pickled tongue. In Philadelphia, a place called Hershel's was gaining a following with its house-smoked pastrami, and each month it seemed like I was hearing about another new-school Jewish deli popping up.

These places were succeeding by tapping into two resonant themes: the universal yearning for comfort food, and a newfound respect for making foods from scratch. It was a return to the basics of old-world cooking. It was nothing short of a born-again deli movement—the Chabad Lubavitch of corned beef on rye!

But for all its innovative spirit, that movement had not breached the walls of that most sacred bastion of Jewish deli culture, New York City. This owed perhaps to a less-than-forgiving environment for young, experimental deli revivalists. New Yorkers of all stripes—from the *New York Times* dining editors to opinionated shoppers complaining about cream cheese prices at Zabar's—had always held fast to the belief that only a New Yorker can truly determine what is good Jewish deli and what isn't. All that DIY stuff going on in Portland or Philly was, as far as the tradition-bound New Yorker was concerned, just a provincial sideshow.

Maybe it's appropriate that it fell on the shoulders of an outsider like Noah to bring the DIY deli movement to New York. While New Yorkers sat waiting to judge the merits of this or that new guy's pastrami and corned beef, Noah showed up with something most of them had never heard of: smoked meat. What was this strange, delicious new thing?

Montreal-style smoked meat—essentially a dry-cured brisket that's been smoked over hardwood—could be called a bastard child of New York–style pastrami, which itself traces its roots to Romania, where the Turkish method of preserving meat (originally mutton) by salting and heavily spicing it with chiles endures to this day. Though the Jewish community in Romania is a sliver of its former self, older cooks I've met there can recall smoked meat's antecedents: namely, goose breast seasoned in the Turkish manner, with paprika, peppers, and other pickling spices, and then cold-smoked and sliced thin. Transferred to the confines of the Lower East Side, goose breast gave way to more plentiful and less expensive beef—especially fatty cuts such as brisket and navel. Pastrami as we know it was born.

Eventually a few of those Romanian butchers and delicatessen men migrated from New York to Montreal, which had its own substantial Romanian Jewish population, and brought their methods with them. Those methods evolved over time, and soon a new strain of old world-style cured meat appeared. In New York City, the seasoning style became sweeter and more fiery, and the meat acquired a black crust of burnt sugar, coriander seed, and peppercorns. Up north, deli men came to rely more on aromatic spices like bay leaf and mustard seed. Nowadays, I like to think of pastrami and smoked meat as two siblings from the same parents.

In Montreal the smoked meat sandwich occupies a place in the local culinary hierarchy that is at least as exalted as pastrami's is in New York. The specialty is equaled in stature only by Montreal's hand-twisted bagels and the French-Canadian diner delicacy known as poutine (French fries topped with cheese curds and gravy). The smoked meat sandwich is always sliced to order, served hot, and garnished with a slick of yellow mustard on seedless rye bread. It is typically accompanied by punchy vinegar coleslaw, double-fried French fries, a Cott black cherry soda, and a few full-sour pickles (my grandmother, a Montrealer, called anything less a "goyish pickle"). Sure, there are other deli staples in Montreal, including the Wilensky special (a pressed salami and bologna sandwich) or Snowdon Deli's bagelach (a cheese-filled pastry), but really, when it comes to Montreal Jewish food, life revolves around smoked meat, whether you get yours at Schwartz's or Ben's or Reuben's or Abie's or Smoked Meat Pete's—all venerable landmarks.

Until Mile End landed in Brooklyn, Montreal-style smoked meat was a mystery to most Americans, who are prevented by law from carrying cured meat over the border. Indeed, it was homesick cravings for his native city's specialty that prompted Noah, newly arrived in New York, to start making his own smoked meat at home in 2008.

I vividly recall the first time I tasted Noah's smoked meat, during a visit to his and Rae's Brooklyn apartment in 2009, half a year or so before Mile End opened. Here was a dark maroon brisket, tender, soft, and plenty fatty. The essence of the spice rub came through perfectly, so that you could taste a hint of the bay leaf, the tickle of garlic, the embers of peppercorn. I knew with one bite that Mile End would change New York's deli scene forever, and that Brooklyn, once again, would be a world-class Jewish delicatessen destination.

In the months that followed, as Mile End's star rose, I was frequently asked by established deli owners from New York and elsewhere whether it lived up to the hype. A few were understandably skeptical and territorial. "I mean, what's so great about Mile End?" asked one owner I'd known for a few years. "Is it that Montreal meat?"

In an era when seemingly every Jewish delicatessen on earth featured a picture of the Statue of Liberty and more New York tchotchkes than a Times Square gift shop, here was a Jewish deli in New York that introduced a different narrative.

....

A large part of it certainly was. In an era when seemingly every Jewish delicatessen on earth featured a picture of the Statue of Liberty and more New York tchotchkes than a Times Square gift shop, here was a Jewish deli in New York that introduced a different narrative. Perhaps, just perhaps, New York's deli lovers could learn something from Montreal's.

But what I often had trouble explaining to those old-school deli men was that Mile End's secret wasn't a secret at all. Their methods and ingredients are out there in the open for all to see. This cookbook stands as irrefutable evidence of that. Nearly everything on Mile End's menu, and in this book, is made from scratch, from the bread the sandwich comes on to the pickles served alongside it. Noah and Rae have nothing to hide, no secret purveyors for their foodstuffs, which are sourced locally from small, organic producers. In this respect, Noah and Rae are simply embracing a more faithful interpretation of Yiddish cooking tradition. Rae's forebearers in Poland didn't have Manischewitz soup mix, and they didn't buy extruded, factory-made pastrami. They did it all from scratch, from simple, honest ingredients that came from nearby. Noah and Rae are

doing it this way, too, not because it's trendy—which it most certainly is—but simply because it tastes better.

The proof is in this book, especially in the amazing DIY deli specialties contained in the section that follows. Yes, you can find really good-quality store-bought versions of most of these foods, but nothing compares to the results you'll get making them from scratch: bigger, fresher flavors; richer textures; and all-around better eating. Whether you're pickling your own lamb's tongues or curing your own lox or slow-smoking your own luscious beef brisket or turkey or chicken, there is something immensely satisfying and pleasurable about this kind of cooking. Only a few of these DIY preparations are big undertakings; many—like the quick-pickled cucumbers or asparagus, or the salt shallots, or the homemade gribenes and schmaltz—are as easy as making grilled cheese. Virtually all of them will spoil you for the store-bought stuff.

If you're still daunted, consider this: The Mile End phenomenon is the work of two people, still in their twenties, with absolutely zero professional cooking experience. That says a lot about Noah and Rae's talents, to be sure, but it also shows how pure and elemental this food is. The DIY recipes on the following pages are within the grasp of anyone who cares to try them. The ingredients are familiar and readily available, and the techniques are straightforward. After all, they were road-tested by generations of Jewish grandmothers.

Meat & Fish

SMOKED MEAT

Noah: Smoked meat is arguably Montreal's most iconic food. Emblematic of the city's working-class immigrant roots, a good smoked meat sandwich is one of the few points of civic pride that both Francophone Nationalists and Anglophone Federalists can agree on wholeheartedly. Stories abound as to who brought smoked meat to Montreal and who's the best at making it, but one thing's for sure: When it comes to symbols of Montreal culture, this delicacy is up there with snow and the Canadiens.

My desire to make this hometown deli specialty from scratch was the genesis for Mile End. As I discovered firsthand, it's a complicated process that can yield inconsistent results unless carried out with great attention to detail. Given the sheer number of variables involved in making a good piece of smoked meat—the particular cut of brisket, the freshness of the curing spices, the efficiency of the smoking method, the skill of the slicer—it's no wonder that so few delicatessens still take on the daily challenge of producing it in-house. The good news is, we've done almost all of the trial and error for you in order to come up with this recipe. We've slightly modified the recipe in use at the deli, which requires custom-grinding eighteen different spices for the curing mixture alone, to make it a little easier for the home cook, but if you follow the steps below, you'll get something very close, and very delicious—pure smoked meat heaven.

Good smoked meat starts, above all else, with a good beef brisket. I highly recommend getting yours from a quality neighborhood butcher. For one thing, he'll be able to trim it to the specifications this recipe calls for. For another, in most cities only a butcher will be able to sell you a whole brisket, as opposed to just the "first cut" or "flat," which is the typical supermarket cut. Whole, intact brisket—comprising both the flat and the smaller, fattier deckle—is what we use at Mile End and is essential for this recipe. A few slices of well-steamed deckle meat in a sandwich can make the difference between a merely satisfying lunch and a religious experience.

recipe continues ➙

Yes, this recipe takes time (nearly two weeks from the start of the cure to the steaming and slicing), but don't be daunted. It's worth it. After all, there aren't really any big secrets to making great smoked meat—just brisket, spice, smoke, and some tender loving care.

You'll find instructions for preparing your smoker on page 18, and a step-by-step primer on slicing smoked brisket on page 23.

FOR THE CURING MIXTURE:

- ¾ cup plus 2 tablespoons Diamond Crystal kosher salt
- 1 tablespoon plus 2 teaspoons pink curing salt
- ½ cup sugar
- 1 pound peeled garlic (about 8–10 heads), minced in a food processor
- 1 cup whole black peppercorns
- 6 tablespoons coriander seeds
- ¼ cup mustard seeds
- 2 tablespoons whole allspice berries, cracked
- 3 tablespoons dehydrated onion
- 3 tablespoons paprika
- 20 dried bay leaves

- 1 12- to 15-pound whole beef brisket, fat cap trimmed to ¼ inch (8–11 pounds post-trim weight)

FOR THE SPICE RUB:

- ¼ cup whole black peppercorns, cracked
- 2 tablespoons coriander seeds
- 1 tablespoon paprika

- 4 pounds oak or other hardwood chips, soaked in cold water for at least 1 hour

CURE THE BRISKET: Combine the curing ingredients in a large bowl. Rub the brisket all over with the curing mixture, patting it down to coat the brisket evenly. Transfer the meat and curing mixture to a brining bag or nonreactive food-grade container with a lid. Let sit, covered, in the refrigerator for 12 days, flipping the brisket over once a day. When the brisket is done curing, rinse it thoroughly under cold running water and then transfer it to a large nonreactive food-grade container filled with enough cold water to submerge the brisket completely. Let soak for 4 hours. (The soaking will temper the saltiness of the meat. It's not necessary to refrigerate it during the soak.)

PREPARE THE BRISKET FOR SMOKING: Combine the spice-rub ingredients in a small bowl. When the brisket is done soaking, remove it from the water, pat it dry with a clean dish towel or paper towels, and transfer the meat, fat-cap side up, to a 10-by-15-inch baking sheet fitted with a rack. Apply the spice rub over the fat-cap side of the brisket. Let it sit at room temperature while you drain your wood chips, pat them dry, and prepare your smoker according to the instructions on page 18.

SMOKE THE BRISKET: When the temperature inside the smoker has reached 215°F and the smoke is flowing steadily, place the brisket on the grill rack, with the fat cap facing up, as far from the heat source as possible. Cook for about 8 hours, monitoring the temperature of the smoker frequently. Also monitor the smoke, adding more presoaked hardwood chips as needed. After 6 hours, start checking the internal temperature of the meat by inserting a meat thermometer into the thickest part of the brisket. It's done when the internal temperature has reached 155°F.

Transfer the brisket to a 10-by-15-inch baking sheet fitted with a rack and let the meat cool overnight, uncovered, in the refrigerator. The brisket can then be wrapped in butcher paper with twine and kept in the refrigerator for up to 10 days.

STEAM THE BRISKET: When you're ready to eat your smoked meat, prepare a stovetop steamer by inserting a rack or a steamer insert into the bottom of a large stockpot. Add enough water to reach the rack or steamer insert, cover, and bring to a boil.

Meanwhile, use a sharp knife to separate the front, tapered part of the brisket from the thicker back end (which also comprises the deckle). The place to make this cut is where the fat cap changes from being very thick to relatively thin. Place the thick back end into the stockpot first, with the fat cap facing up, and then lay the tapered portion on top of that (also with the fat cap facing up). Cover and steam, adding more water to the bottom of the pot as necessary, until the tapered portion of the brisket is very tender but still firm enough to be transferred to a cutting board using a carving fork, 1½ to 2 hours. Continue steaming the back end of the brisket until it reaches the same level of tenderness, about 1½ hours more.

Slice the brisket following the instructions on page 23, and see page 121 for sandwich-assembly instructions.

MAKES ROUGHLY 60 PERCENT
OF ORIGINAL WEIGHT

Chopping oak for smoking

BEEF SALAMI

Noah: Beef salami has been a staple at my parents' home for as long as I can remember. As a kid, I'd slice off a few pieces after school, after hockey practice, before bed, even for breakfast. Even now I can't stay away: I'll steal a piece right off the griddle during a hectic brunch service at Mile End.

Though beef salami has seen better days—your average Jewish deli probably gets it from a large factory producer—I've always thought of this food as an unsung hero of deli. At Mile End, we use a blend of deckle meat from the brisket and short ribs to produce a fatty, garlicky, paprika-laced thing of beauty. Whether you fry it up with eggs in a skillet (see page 109) or griddle it and press it into an onion roll (see page 122), this is a salami with haute credentials and blue-collar roots.

Frankly, there's a reason most delis don't make their own beef salami; it is very hard to do. It took me a long time, and plenty of mistakes, to get ours to where it is today. Stuffing a large encased meat product is something of an art, as is the incrementally graded low-temperature smoking this recipe calls for. So don't get discouraged if you don't nail it on your first attempt. Keep trying, and—if you're half as serious about salami as I am—spring for good equipment. Specifically: a piston-style crank stuffer and a semi-professional smoker with built-in temperature controls.

2 2½-inch-diameter collagen casings, cut into 18-inch lengths	1 tablespoon Hungarian paprika
3 tablespoons black peppercorns	1 tablespoon granulated onion
2 tablespoons yellow mustard seeds	10 garlic cloves, finely minced
1 teaspoon fennel seeds	2½ pounds ground fatty brisket
½ teaspoon cumin seeds	2½ pounds ground beef short rib
3 tablespoons Diamond Crystal kosher salt	Butcher's twine
1 teaspoon pink curing salt	Oak wood chips, or a blend of hickory and apple wood chips

Soak the casings in room-temperature water for at least 30 minutes. Working in batches, use a spice grinder to grind the peppercorns, mustard seeds, fennel seeds, and cumin seeds to a powder. Combine the ground spices in a bowl with the salts, Hungarian paprika, granulated onion, and minced garlic.

recipe continues ➜

Place the beef in a large bowl and break it up a bit with your hands. Add the spice mixture and gently work it into the beef until the spices are evenly distributed throughout the meat; do not overmix (that will smear the fat and create an undesired paste-like consistency).

Prepare your sausage stuffer or the sausage-stuffing attachment of a standing mixer. Remove the sausage casings from the water bath and pat them dry with a paper towel. Take one length of casing and very tightly tie off and seal one end of it, pulling the twine very taut and making multiple knots. Trim the excess twine.

Add meat to the receptacle of the stuffer and start cranking it through until just a small amount protrudes through the mouth of the stuffer. Place the open end of the casing over the mouth of the stuffer tube and thread the casing onto it fully, so that the tied end of the casing is pressing up against the protruding meat. Gripping the casing close to the mouth of the stuffer tube, start cranking the meat into the casing, keeping a firm enough grip that very little air is allowed inside the casing. Continue stuffing until only 3 or 4 inches of unfilled casing are left. If using a casing that is larger in diameter than the stuffing tube, try rotating the casing while stuffing for more even distribution.

Take a couple of feet of twine and, cinching closed the unsealed end of the casing firmly to push out any air, use your other hand to start wrapping the twine very tightly around the cinched casing. As you wrap the twine, work inward to choke up on the casing. After wrapping the twine 10 or so times, tie it off very tightly and trim the excess twine.

Using a toothpick or skewer, poke tiny holes in the casing where you're able to see any air pockets, especially near the ends. Repeat with the remaining meat and casings. Refrigerate the salamis overnight, uncovered.

COOK THE SALAMIS: Prepare your smoker according to the instructions on page 18. If you're not using a two-chamber smoker or a fancy temperature-controlled unit, we recommend positioning a tray of ice between the heat source and the cooking surface to cool the smoke (you'll need to replace the ice often). Insert your probe thermometer into the salami and cook in four stages: 1½ hours at 110°F; 1½ hours at 125°F; 1½ hours at 140°F; and, finally, 1 hour at 155°F, until the internal temperature of the salami reaches 145°F.

Transfer the cooked salamis to an ice bath for 60 minutes to halt the cooking and to prevent casing shrinkage. Refrigerate for at least one week before serving.

The salamis will keep in the refrigerator for up to four more weeks, developing a deeper flavor over time.

MAKES 2 SALAMIS, ABOUT 2 POUNDS EACH

CORNED BEEF

Rae: Corned beef—smoked meat's wet-cured, unsmoked sister—was never really a part of Montreal deli tradition, but I felt we just had to have it on the Mile End menu. Like any New Yorker I know, Jewish or not, I grew up eating it and loving it. Corned beef is quintessential New York delicatessen, and this recipe is about as traditional as you get. It's easy, too: You use the same aromatics, in the exact same amounts, for the cooking liquid as you do for the curing.

FOR CURING THE BEEF:
- 20 cups water
- 2¼ cups Diamond Crystal kosher salt
- ⅔ cup sugar
- 2 tablespoons pink curing salt
- 4 garlic cloves, peeled
- 2 teaspoons coriander seeds
- 10 allspice berries
- 2 teaspoons yellow mustard seeds
- 4 whole cloves
- 1 cinnamon stick
- 2 stalks of celery
- ½ carrot
- ½ small onion
- 2 sprigs of thyme
- 3 fresh bay leaves
- 1 5-pound first-cut brisket

FOR COOKING THE BEEF:
- 4 garlic cloves, peeled
- 2 teaspoons whole coriander
- 10 allspice berries
- 2 teaspoons yellow mustard seeds
- 4 whole cloves
- 1 cinnamon stick
- 2 stalks of celery
- ½ carrot
- ½ small onion
- 2 sprigs of thyme
- 3 bay leaves

MAKE THE CURING SOLUTION: Combine all the curing ingredients except the brisket in a large nonreactive pot and bring to a boil; adjust the heat and simmer, stirring until the sugar is dissolved. Transfer the curing liquid to the refrigerator and let it sit until chilled. Then add the brisket to the pot, weighing it down with a plate or other heavy object so that the meat remains fully submerged. Refrigerate, covered, for 5 days.

COOK THE BEEF: Fill the pot with enough water to fully cover the meat by an inch or two. Then add all the cooking ingredients. Bring to a boil over high heat, then adjust the heat and cook at a low simmer until fork-tender, 3 to 4 hours.

MAKES 3½ TO 4 POUNDS

ROAST BEEF

Noah: At the deli we use a chuck-eye roll of wagyu beef, which is a cross of Angus and Japanese Kobe and has incredible marbling. We recommend looking for the best-quality top round or eye round—the two most popular roast-beef cuts—you can find. This is classic roast beef: cooked with no aromatics, it's just earthy, meaty, and beautiful. Make a pan gravy with the drippings if you want, and serve the beef warm with Pickled Horseradish (page 86), or serve it cold and sliced thin as a lunch meat.

1 **7-pound beef chuck-eye roast**
   Canola oil
   Diamond Crystal kosher salt and freshly ground black pepper

Preheat the oven to 500°F. Rub the beef all over with oil and sprinkle it very generously with salt and pepper. Place the beef in a roasting pan fitted with a rack and cook for 1 hour for rare. If using an eye round, roast for only 30 minutes. Then, without opening the oven door, turn off the heat and let the roast continue to cook for another hour or so, until a thermometer inserted into the center of the roast reads 120°F. Let cool for 1 hour. Slice as thinly as possible.

MAKES ENOUGH FOR 12 TO 15 SANDWICHES; SERVES 6 TO 8 AS AN ENTRÉE

Joel Bukiewicz
Knife-maker & owner, CUT Brooklyn

How to Love Your Knife So It'll Love You Back

MY NAME IS JOEL BUKIEWICZ, AND I MAKE KNIVES. I learned to make them when I was living in a small town down in Georgia trying to write a novel. Turns out I'm a lot better at making knives than I am at writing fiction. Now I have a small storefront in Gowanus, Brooklyn, that's open two days a week; the rest of the time I'm in my workshop making knives, all handcrafted from sheets of custom-made steel. I make both stainless steel knives and carbon steel knives; carbon steel often sharpens more easily but requires a little more care and maintenance. I make knives for chefs, for nonchefs, and for anyone who cares about the tools they use in the kitchen. The knives I build are meant to last a lifetime.

You develop a strong muscle memory with the tools that you use every day; they become an extension of your body. So find a knife that feels right. Shop at a place where they'll let you test-drive the knives. Find a knife that appeals to you aesthetically as well as physically; it should be something you'll be interested in caring for, something with which you'll want to develop a relationship. The two most important knives in any drawer are the chef's knife—the one I use at home is a 10-inch carbon steel one I made myself—and a thin, well made paring knife. I use a petty knife for paring, which is like a mini 5-inch version of a chef's knife. It's small enough for intricate work but long and tall enough to use on a board for small vegetables like shallots and garlic.

Of all the tools in your kitchen, the knife is the one you have the most physical and kinetic relationship with. So get to know it intimately; know when it's in need. First and foremost, that means keeping it sharp. A lot of people are crazy about Japanese knives these days, and most of the knives coming out of Japan are beautifully made tools, but most also need to be hand sharpened on water stones, because the blade has been left extremely hard during the tempering process, and they'll chip on a microscopic level if honed on a sharpening steel. And learning to sharpen well on a water stone is a lifetime endeavor, an art form. For most knives, there are a lot of great inexpensive honing products out there. I like the steels made by Messermeister. Their steels are machined super cleanly, without any irregularities, so you get a nice even "tooth" to your edge. My idea of the perfect edge for a kitchen knife is just enough tooth to bite into the skin of a soft tomato, but enough polish that it'll hold onto that edge for a long time. I stay away from diamond sharpening tools; they tend to be too aggressive. I love a cleanly machined medium-grade steel or a quality ceramic hone.

When you're sharpening, find the right angle—somewhere between fifteen and twenty degrees usually does the trick. You want to stroke from heel to tip, with even, light pressure. Those guys on TV who are like ding-ding-ding-ding-ding, really fast? That's just scary, and there's really no need for it. Stroke slow and smooth, letting the knife's weight do the work. When you're done, look straight down at the edge in good light, moving the blade back and forth; if there are any spots along the edge that are returning light, that are shiny, those are areas where the edge has sort of flopped over. Give it a few more strokes to get those spots out. Ideally you want to hone your knife before every use, or at least every two or three uses.

Wash your knife with soap and water, that's it. Never put it in the dishwasher. The issue with the dishwasher is not a rust thing, but the damage it does to the adhesive that keeps your handles on: That adhesive degrades under heat. When you're washing, move your dishcloth or sponge across the blade lengthwise and gently, in single strokes always aimed away from the edge, from handle to tip. It's when people start scrubbing and moving their hand back toward the edge that they cut themselves. I've given a few knives to people as gifts, and they've cut the hell out of themselves—it's always while washing. Dry your knife carefully and put it away; don't toss it in a dish rack or ever in the sink where it'll bang up against glass and steel.

Finally, get a good end-grain wood cutting board for a cutting surface. It'll always be kind to your knife. Stay away from marble or glass, for God's sake. Those things give me the shivers. It's like driving your sports car on its rims. And if you've got to cut through bone or pry apart chunks of frozen food, break out an old butter knife or a cleaver or even a hacksaw if you have to. Don't use your chef's knife, with its thin, beautiful edge. Because that's not what it's made to do, and really, it's no way to treat a loved one.

DUCK & MAPLE SAUSAGE

Rae: Duck has long been considered a delicacy in European Jewish cooking, but you don't see it much in Jewish home cooking these days. I've always thought that's a shame—it's so rich and fatty and flavorful. Which is why it works great in a sausage. At Mile End we serve them with fried eggs, Maple Baked Beans (page 81), and thick-cut Challah (page 177), a breakfast I have seen Noah polish off in mere minutes.

Meat (skin and fat removed and reserved) from 1 6-pound Long Island duck (about 1½ pounds)

¾ pound of the reserved duck fat and skin

3½ teaspoons Diamond Crystal kosher salt

2 tablespoons minced shallots

3 tablespoons plus 1 teaspoon maple syrup

1 tablespoon soy-protein concentrate (optional)

1½ teaspoons dried ginger

1½ teaspoons rubbed dried sage

1 teaspoon freshly ground white pepper

2 teaspoons Spanish smoked paprika

5 or 6 ice cubes

Preflushed 26-millimeter lamb casings (if making links instead of patties)

Vegetable oil (optional)

Cut the meat, fat, and skin into 1-inch pieces and combine with the remaining ingredients except the ice cubes, casings, and oil. Toss well to incorporate all the ingredients. Refrigerate for 3 to 4 hours, or as long as overnight.

Meanwhile, place your meat-grinding attachment in the freezer. When ready to grind, add the ice cubes to the meat mixture, and pass it through the coarse die of the grinder. Reserve half of the coarsely ground mixture in the refrigerator while you pass the other half through the medium die of the grinder. Add the more finely ground mixture to the coarsely ground mixture and fold gently to combine. If you're not making links, form the sausage mixture into about 15 patties.

If you're making links, soak the lamb casings in slightly warm water for 1 hour and then, using a sausage stuffer, pipe the sausage mixture into the casings, twisting off 6-inch links as you go. Prick the casings with a skewer or toothpick where any air pockets appear.

Cook the sausage links or patties in a dry pan or skillet—or with a small amount of oil, if you like—over medium heat until cooked through and browned all over. (You can refrigerate the uncooked sausage mixture for up to 3 days, but do not freeze it.)

MAKES ABOUT 15 LINKS OR PATTIES

CHOPPED LIVER

Rae: This version of the classic Jewish comfort food has converted more than a few nonbelievers; it even worked for me, someone who never liked chopped liver growing up. It's got a luscious flavor and texture, and the crunchy, salty garnishes put it over the top. We swap pickled onions for the traditional fried topping for a needed brightness, and our Pletzel (page 184) makes for the perfect vehicle. I recommend using a meat grinder, but if you don't have one, pulsing the ingredients in a food processor works too.

½ cup Schmaltz (page 91)

3 cups chopped onion

1 pound chicken livers

1 fresh bay leaf

1 sprig of thyme

4 large eggs, boiled, peeled, and coarsely chopped

1 teaspoon quatre-épices (equal parts white pepper, ginger, cloves, and cinnamon)

Diamond Crystal kosher salt and freshly ground black pepper

3 scallions, sliced into thin rings

FOR SERVING:

Sieved egg (a peeled hard-boiled egg pressed through the coarse holes of a box grater)

Pickled Red Onions (page 66)

Gribenes (page 91)

Pletzel (page 184)

Heat the schmaltz in a large sauté pan over medium-high heat. Add the onion and fry until the edges start to brown. Add the chicken livers, bay leaf, and thyme. Lower the heat slightly and cook, stirring often, until the livers are just barely cooked through, about 10 minutes. Set the liver-and-onion mixture aside and let it cool to room temperature. Remove the bay leaf and thyme sprig and add the eggs and quatre-épices. Season with salt and pepper to taste. Pass the mixture through the small die of a meat grinder, or pulse in a food processor until coarsely chopped. Fold in the scallions and adjust the salt and pepper to taste. Garnish with the sieved egg, pickled red onions, and gribenes; serve with pletzel.

SERVES 8 AS AN APPETIZER

PICKLED LAMB'S TONGUE

Rae: Noah jokes that tongue is "nature's hot dog"—the meat just has that smooth, emulsified texture that's similar to a good frankfurter. It fell out of favor for a while as a deli specialty, maybe because of the gross-out factor, but nose-to-tail eating is more popular now, and tongue, so flavorful, is getting the love again. For the appetizer we serve at the deli (see page 144), we like to use pickled lamb's tongue instead of the more standard (and much bigger) beef or veal tongue because it's less rich and has a sweet gaminess. The meat takes really well to pickling, and with lamb you can do a lot of tongues in one shot. We slice the pickled lamb's tongue lengthwise and sear it, which makes for a really elegant presentation, but you can slice it into rounds as you would a deli meat, for sandwiches or as the old-school star of a cold-cuts plate.

8 cups water
1 cup Diamond Crystal kosher salt
2 teaspoons pink curing salt (optional)
3 garlic cloves, peeled
1½ tablespoons coriander seeds
1½ tablespoons black peppercorns

1½ teaspoons yellow mustard seeds
3 fresh bay leaves
2 to 3 sprigs of thyme
1½ cups (packed) light brown sugar
6 lamb tongues (about 1¼ to 1½ pounds total)

MAKE THE BRINE: Combine the water, kosher salt, pink curing salt, garlic, coriander, peppercorns, mustard seeds, bay leaves, and thyme in a large nonreactive pot and bring to a boil. Remove from the heat, add the brown sugar, and stir until the sugar has completely dissolved. Cover the pot and refrigerate overnight. Add the tongues to the chilled brining solution, cover, and refrigerate for 5 days.

Remove the tongues from the brining solution and discard the solution (along with the spices, garlic, and herbs).

COOK THE TONGUES: Return the tongues to a clean nonreactive pot and add enough cold water to cover them completely. Bring to a boil, then reduce the heat and simmer, skimming any foam off the top from time to time, for 1½ hours. Use a small plate or pot lid to keep the tongues submerged for even cooking.

Check the tongues for doneness by inserting a wooden skewer all the way through a tongue and pulling it back out again. If it slides out with no resistance, the tongue is done. If the skewer pulls the tongue up with it, cook a little longer.

Transfer the tongues and their cooking liquid to a baking dish that's big enough to allow the tongues to sit in a single layer without touching. Let the tongues sit in their liquid until they're just cool enough to handle but still quite hot, then use a paring knife to peel off the inedible white membrane covering the tongue. (The hotter the tongues are, the easier they will be to peel; we recommend using rubber gloves so you can handle them while they are still pretty hot.)

Return the tongues to their cooking liquid, cover, and refrigerate overnight. The pickled tongues will keep in their liquid for about 1 week.

MAKES 6

ORDER YOUR RIB ROAST for XMAS TODAY! $20 /#

Tom Mylan
Co-founder, The Meat Hook, Brooklyn

It's Not Fun Without the Fat!

ON BRISKET: A brisket should have a lot of fat on it. I mean, it's a brisket! If you don't see that thick cap of fat and rich marbling, forget it. Don't buy a brisket that's pink; you want one that's a nice, dark ruby red. Not to get all science-y, but that red color comes from a compound called myoglobin; the more myoglobin in the muscle tissue, the more beefy and rich that meat is going to taste. That said, purple is not good. Purple is an indicator that the beef is really old and the texture is just going to be totally screwed, or that it's from a dairy animal or some other cow that was not raised for beef.

ON LAMB: When you're doing cured preparations like bacon or pastrami, lamb is fine, but why not try mutton? It's fattier, cheaper, and more flavorful. Whenever you're doing anything cured, the more mature the animal, the better: The whole point of this kind of preserving has traditionally been to add value to tougher or stronger-tasting cuts of meat that wouldn't take well to fast cooking. You need meat that can stand up to the flavor of the cure and the smoke, and you need that fat. It's not fun without the fat! Basically, you're taking a cow's ear and turning it into a silk purse—or I guess it's a sow's ear, but obviously that doesn't apply to Jewish deli cooking.

ON TURKEYS AND CHICKENS: This is going to make a lot of people mad at me, but I think that heritage-breed turkey is kind of bullshit overrated. Unless you're going to go straight to wild turkey, I don't think heritage-breed is that much more flavorful, and it's a lot tougher. It's also a lot more expensive and difficult to cook. I got a heritage-breed turkey for Thanksgiving a few years ago, thinking I was doing the right thing—I could see Alice Waters patting me on the head and saying, "You've done well, my son"—but it just wasn't that good! So with turkey, I'm going to say to just buy an organic one, because you don't want the hormones and antibiotics, but other than that, go for the broad-breasted white.

My views on chicken are a different matter. Spend the extra money and get a fully pasture-raised bird. And watch out: The label "free-range" can be, frankly, meaningless—it can indicate as little as that the birds can come outside of their coops once in a while to peck around. You want a chicken that has lived all of its life outside, eating grass and bugs. They're just so much more delicious, and they give a whole new meaning to that lame expression "tastes like chicken," which actually reflects the typical supermarket chicken that has pretty much all of its flavor bred out of it. You want to cook a pasture-raised bird really slowly, at not more than 325°F, except maybe to blast it at the end to crisp up the skin.

ON CHICKEN LIVERS: The big thing with buying chicken livers is you don't want any greenish tinge to them—if there's the slightest bit of green, don't buy them. They're off, done. You're looking for a nice ruby red color—like with beef brisket—but not too dark. They should look shiny and fresh and vibrant and vital. We go through twenty to thirty pounds of chicken livers a week. You wouldn't believe the variety of people who buy them: Jewish grandmothers, old Chinese ladies, beautiful young Polish women. And the Russians! These Russian gangster types come into the shop and wave their hand in front of the case: "I'll take all the steaks you got. Oh, and a couple pounds of chicken liver."

ON KNOWING YOUR BUTCHER: When you go to the butcher shop, you're paying a little bit more in order to get better-quality and better-sourced meat, but you're also paying for knowledge. Every person who works behind the counter of any reputable butcher shop almost certainly knows more than you do about meat. You could be the biggest food nerd in the world, but you're still not going to have the practical knowledge of people who cut up meat all day long and go home to cook it every different way. So go in there with an open mind. I love a customer who comes into my shop and says something like, "I want to make pastrami, or maybe roast beef, or maybe corned beef—I haven't decided." To that person I'd say, "Oh, man, get boneless short ribs, and make that into pastrami, because it's really good—but only if you're going to serve it hot," and so on. Look, I stumbled into this line of work by accident—I started out as a pizza cook, for God's sake—but the truth is, being a butcher is a calling, and you might as well throw your money out the window if you're not going to tap into that.

SMOKED TURKEY

Noah: A good primer for the world of smoked foods, turkey is readily found in grocery stores, does not require intense or complicated brining, and cooks to a beautiful golden doneness in relatively little time. This recipe produces a bird that's both basic enough to fill a week's worth of lunches and delicious enough to impress your friends and family on a Thanksgiving table, especially when served with our Cranberry Sauce (page 73). We use it for our Grandpa sandwich (page 130) and for big old kitchen-sink salads. You can even freestyle this recipe by concocting your own glaze or rub for the turkey in the step between brining and smoking.

18 cups water
½ cup Diamond Crystal kosher salt
½ cup sugar
6 to 8 garlic cloves, peeled
1½ tablespoons black peppercorns
1½ tablespoons juniper berries
½ tablespoon yellow mustard seeds

½ tablespoon coriander seeds
8 fresh bay leaves
1 8- to 10-pound bone-in turkey breast
   Cherry wood chips, apple wood chips, or other fruit wood chips
½ lemon
1 tablespoon coarsely ground black pepper

MAKE THE BRINING SOLUTION: In a large nonreactive pot, combine 6 cups of the water, the salt, and sugar and bring to a boil; remove from the heat. In a separate large nonreactive pot, combine the remaining 12 cups of water and the garlic, peppercorns, juniper berries, mustard seeds, coriander seeds, and bay leaves. Pour the boiled salt-sugar solution into the second pot; stir to combine. Place the turkey in the brining solution; weigh the turkey down with a plate or other heavy object so that it remains fully submerged. Cover and refrigerate for 3 days.

Remove the turkey from the brining solution and pat it dry with paper towels. Let the turkey sit, uncovered, in the refrigerator overnight.

COOK THE TURKEY: Soak the wood chips in water for 30 minutes, then drain and pat them dry. Prepare your smoker according to the instructions on page 18. When the temperature inside the smoker has reached 200°F and the wood chips are smoking steadily, add the turkey, maintain the temperature at 200°F, and let smoke for 3 hours. Meanwhile, preheat the oven to 325°F. Transfer the turkey to a roasting pan and rub it all over with the lemon half and the black pepper. Then roast in the oven until a thermometer inserted into the thickest part of the breast reads 165°F, about 2½ hours. Let rest at least 20 minutes before slicing.

The smoked turkey will keep in the refrigerator for up to one week.

MAKES 6 TO 8 POUNDS

SMOKED CHICKEN BREAST

Noah: We sear these breasts to make our Spring Chicken entrée (page 143). Buy whole chickens and have the butcher cut them up so that you can use the legs and thighs to make the Chicken Confit (page 77).

16 cups water	4 sprigs of thyme
¾ cup Diamond Crystal kosher salt	3 sprigs of rosemary
5 tablespoons sugar	8 to 10 sage leaves
4 garlic cloves, peeled	2 whole bone-in chicken breasts with wing joints attached (about 1½ to 2 pounds each)
Juice of 1 lemon	
¼ cup black peppercorns	
3 dried árbol chiles	Cherry wood chips, apple wood chips, or other fruit wood chips
3 fresh bay leaves	

MAKE THE BRINING SOLUTION: Bring the water, salt, and sugar to a boil in a large nonreactive pot. Remove from the heat, stir, and let cool. Add the remaining ingredients except the wood chips to the pot, weighing the chicken breasts down with a plate or other heavy object to keep them submerged. Cover the pot and refrigerate for 3 days.

Remove the chicken breasts from the brining solution, pat them dry, and let them sit, uncovered, in the refrigerator overnight.

COOK THE CHICKEN: Soak the wood chips in water for 30 minutes, then drain and pat them dry. Prepare your smoker according to the instructions on page 18. When the temperature inside the smoker has reached 200°F and the wood chips are smoking steadily, add the chicken and let smoke. Maintain the temperature at 200°F until a thermometer inserted into the thickest part of the breast reads 150°F, about 45 minutes to 1 hour.

When the chicken breasts are cool enough to handle, remove the breasts from the rib cage: Working with one whole breast at a time, locate the keel bone running down the centerline of the breast. Using a sharp boning knife, make a smooth, deep cut along one side of the keel bone, cutting as close to the bone as possible, until the tip of your blade hits the rib cage. Then, using your fingers to gently pry the meat outward from the keel bone, begin cutting the meat away from the rib cage using the tip of the knife.

Feel for the edge of the rib bones with your fingers, so that you leave as little meat on the rib cage as possible. Work your way from the neck end to the rump end; when you've reached the joint where the wing attaches to the rest of the body, gently pull the breast and its wing away from the carcass until the joint pops. Carefully cut the breast and its wing away at the joint. Repeat with the other half of the breast, and again with both halves of the second whole breast.

The smoked, de-caged breasts will keep in the refrigerator for up to one week.

MAKES 4 PORTIONS

LAMB BACON

Noah: We're always looking for alternatives to pork at Mile End, and this dry-cured lamb breast was an amazing meat discovery for me. You can use lamb bacon in pretty much any dish you'd use standard bacon or pancetta for: Italian peasant soups, potato salads, meat braises, pasta dishes, whatever. We finish our lamb bacon in a smoker, though at home I've cooked it in the oven and gotten great results; it just has a milder flavor. You can store the bacon in the fridge for many weeks.

5 tablespoons Diamond Crystal kosher salt

2 teaspoons pink curing salt

3 tablespoons (packed) dark brown sugar

4 dried bay leaves, crushed

1 tablespoon plus 1 teaspoon freshly ground black pepper

1 1½- to 2-pound boneless lamb breast, with silver skin intact

Cherry wood chips, apple wood chips, or other fruit wood chips

MAKE THE RUB: Combine the salts, brown sugar, bay leaves, and pepper in a bowl and transfer to a large plate or a baking dish. Dredge the lamb breast in the rub and massage it into the surface of the lamb. (You'll probably have some rub left over.) Shake off any excess rub and let the meat sit, covered, in the refrigerator for 5 days, turning the lamb over once a day.

Rinse the lamb breast thoroughly, pat it dry with paper towels, and allow it to sit uncovered in the refrigerator overnight.

COOK THE LAMB BACON: Soak the wood chips in water for 30 minutes, then drain and them pat dry. Prepare your smoker according to the instructions on page 18. When the temperature inside the smoker has reached 200°F and the wood chips are smoking steadily, add the lamb, and let smoke. Maintain the temperature at 200°F at least until a thermometer inserted into the center of the meat reads 160°F. This will take about 2 hours, but we recommend smoking for 3, as longer cooking enhances the quality of the bacon. Allow the bacon to cool completely in the fridge and store, wrapped, for up to 1 month.

TIP: *The size of lamb breasts can vary quite a bit, so be sure to buy yours deboned or boneless. A bone-in breast will lose 30 to 35 percent of its weight upon deboning.*

NOTE: *If you'd prefer to use an oven, preheat to 200°F and cook for 3 hours.*

MAKES 1 TO 1½ POUNDS

SMOKED MACKEREL

Rae: When we were putting together the Mile End menu, Noah and I searched long and hard to find a smoked fish that was similar to sable but wasn't as fatty and expensive. Eventually we found our holy grail: Spanish mackerel. Though it's less oily than sable or herring, its flesh stands up to smoking without drying out. It's an all-around great East Coast fish, and it's highly sustainable. You can eat this smoked mackerel as a main dinner course, or do like we do at Mile End and put it on a kaiser roll with some sweet Cider-Mustard Glaze and Tartar Sauce (see page 131 for the full sandwich recipe).

8 cups water
½ cup Diamond Crystal kosher salt
¼ cup sugar
3 whole cloves
1 tablespoon yellow mustard seeds
2 fresh bay leaves

Spanish mackerel fillets with skin (about 1½ pounds)
Canola oil for the grill grate
Cherry wood chips, apple wood chips, or other fruit wood chips

MAKE THE BRINING SOLUTION: Combine the water, salt, and sugar in a large nonreactive pot and bring to a boil, stirring until the salt and sugar have dissolved, then remove from the heat. Add the cloves, mustard seeds, and bay leaves and let the mixture cool to room temperature. Add the mackerel fillets and let them soak in the brine for 60 to 90 minutes.

Transfer the fillets to a draining rack and refrigerate them, uncovered, overnight; by morning, a taut, slightly sticky layer (called a pellicle) should form on the surface of the fish.

COOK THE MACKEREL: Soak the wood chips in water for 30 minutes, then drain and pat them dry. Prepare your smoker according to the instructions on page 18. Be sure to grease the smoker grate with oil before cooking. When the temperature inside the smoker has reached 200°F and the wood chips are smoking steadily, add the fillets, and let the fish smoke until cooked through and the flesh flakes easily when prodded with a knife, 40 to 60 minutes. Before serving, use a pair of tweezers or needle-nose pliers to remove the pin bones from the fillets. The fillets will keep in the fridge for up to 1 week.

MAKES 6 SANDWICHES OR 4 ENTRÉES

Left: Curing Salmon (for Lox); *Above:* Pickled Belly Lox

LOX

Noah: We use this salt-cured salmon recipe for two of our signature breakfast dishes, the Beauty (page 98) and the Mish-Mash (page 109), but it's great for all sorts of other preparations.

Curing salmon is all about the fat. We use king salmon for making lox at the deli, and always the farmed variety, not wild. That's because wild salmon tends to be too lean for curing. Too little fat will cause the salt mixture to "burn" the surface of the salmon and stop the cure from penetrating. Allowing the fillet to rest for a day after rinsing off the curing mixture enables the fish to continue "cooking"—that is, it lets the curing compounds distribute themselves evenly throughout the salmon. Using good kosher salt for this recipe is absolutely essential.

⅓ cup whole black peppercorns
⅔ cup sugar
1 cup Diamond Crystal kosher salt
1 bunch of dill
1 2-pound boneless king salmon fillet, with skin

Combine the peppercorns, sugar, and salt in a bowl and stir to combine. Place 2 or 3 sprigs of the dill in the bottom of a nonreactive baking dish, and sprinkle about ¼ cup of the salt mixture evenly over the bottom of the dish.

Make 2 or 3 shallow cuts in the skin of the salmon fillet. Place the salmon, skin side down, on top of the salt and dill, and place a few more sprigs of dill on top of the salmon. Sprinkle the salmon all over with another ¼ cup of the salt mixture. Reserve the remaining salt mixture. Loosely cover the baking dish with plastic wrap and refrigerate it overnight.

Carefully pour off any liquid that has accumulated in the baking dish. Add another ¼ cup of the salt mixture to the bottom of the dish, and sprinkle ¼ cup more over the salmon. Replace the dill sprigs with new ones if they've wilted. Cover the dish and refrigerate overnight.

Repeat this process 2 more times over 2 more days.

On the fifth day, remove the salmon, rinse it thoroughly, and pat it dry with paper towels. Place the salmon on a small drying rack set inside a clean baking dish or over a couple of layers of paper towels. Refrigerate, uncovered, overnight.

To serve, slice very thinly and carefully at a shallow angle, working from the front of the fillet toward the tail.

MAKES ABOUT 1½ POUNDS

PICKLED BELLY LOX

Rae: Luscious, fatty salmon bellies take really nicely to pickling. At Mile End, pickled belly lox gets served on its own as a melt-in-your-mouth appetizer or as part of a brunch spread; if you add some simply dressed field greens, you've got a healthy, high-protein lunch. Ask for fresh salmon bellies from your fishmonger—you'll typically need to order them ahead, and ask for the skin to be removed—then cure the bellies as you would for the Lox recipe on the opposite page before pickling them. The pickling brine is the same one used for the Pickled Red Onions on page 66.

> Cured bellies from 2 salmon
> (4 pieces; see opposite page for curing instructions)
> 2 small white onions, thinly sliced
> 6 sprigs of dill
> 1 quart onion-pickling brine
> (see Pickled Red Onions recipe, page 66),
> unstrained and kept warm

Rinse the cured bellies, cut them into 2- to 3-inch lengths, and layer them in a nonreactive container (any glass or plastic container will do) along with the onions and dill. Pour the warm brine, whole spices and all, over the fish. Place the open container in the refrigerator, covering it after the mixture has chilled. Let the bellies marinate for 2 to 3 days before serving.

SERVES ABOUT 6 AS AN APPETIZER

Niki Russ Federman
Fourth-generation co-owner,
Russ & Daughters, New York City

An Appetizing Life

I'M NIKI RUSS FEDERMAN, the fourth-generation co-owner of Russ & Daughters on the Lower East Side. We're one of the last Jewish appetizing stores left in New York City, or anywhere for that matter. Russ & Daughters was founded by my great-grandfather Joel Russ, born Yoel Russ, an immigrant from what is now part of Poland. He started with a barrel of herring on Orchard Street, which at the turn of the last century was the central marketplace of the Lower East Side, where pushcart vendors catered to the immense wave of Eastern European immigrants coming to the new world. That was 1908. Within a few years he'd worked his way up from barrel to pushcart, and then, in 1914, from pushcart to storefront. We've been here ever since.

The store has had various names through the years; it was J. Russ National Appetizing for a while, and then, in the '20s or thereabouts, it was Russ's Cut-Rate Appetizing. The "Cut-Rate" was meant to set the shop apart from the scores of other appetizing stores that existed at that time all over New York City—pretty much in any neighborhood that had a Jewish enclave. In those neighborhoods, you'd always have your delicatessen, which sold cured and smoked meats, and you'd have your appetizing store, for fish and dairy, in keeping with Jewish dietary laws. Up until the 1940s, when Jewish immigration started to taper off, the Lower East Side alone probably had about thirty appetizing stores, and I don't know how many delicatessens.

My great-grandfather didn't have any sons, but he had three daughters: Hattie, Ida, and Anne. Anne is my grandmother. She and Hattie are in their nineties now and still going. Hattie was probably twelve when she started working here, and her sisters soon followed. My great-grandfather, who wasn't much of a people person, realized pretty quickly that having three cute girls selling herring was great for business. So in 1935, he changed the name of the store to Russ & Daughters. People thought he'd lost it. Why would you ruin a reputable business with that kind of name? But the name held, and eventually my father, who'd been a lawyer for ten years, quit his practice and came into the business. Today my cousin Josh and I run it.

Appetizing stores came out of the Eastern European tradition of *forshpayz*, which is the Yiddish term for cold appetizers that start a meal. Shops like ours sold ready-to-eat foods that had been cured or pickled or smoked, especially fish—basically the kinds of things you'd put on a bagel or a bialy, the things you could eat right away when you got home from synagogue. Today we sell all sorts of different smoked and cured fish, such as smoked salmon and herring and lox, plus spreads, bagels, bialys, and more—quintessential appetizing fare. There's a sweet side to appetizing too, and so we have a lot of classic treats, like black-and-white cookies, rugelach, and babka. It's that combination of the sweet, the savory, the smoky, the salty, the pickled, and the cured, all coming together, that embodies the beauty of appetizing.

I love when people walk into our store and say, "I remember coming here fifty years ago!" The truth is, the shop doesn't look all that different. In a place like New York, where everything is changing all the time, to have a place where you can feel that continuity is really special. For many people, these foods represent what it means to be from New York, and to be Jewish in New York. This is the food that you have when a baby is born, or for a bar mitzvah or a wedding, or for sitting shiva. It's comfort food.

We get customers who come in straight from the airport after a trip, stopping in to get their belly lox or smoked sable before even going home. I know of more than a few people who've eaten Russ & Daughters as their last meal, literally. I have a customer I've known for a long time who lives in California. For a while she was coming to New York once a month to visit her mother, who was ill. On one of her visits, the daughter came in and bought a whole bunch of stuff. She told me that her mother didn't have much time left and that this was all she wanted to eat. The daughter later told me that her mother was noshing on our smoked fish and bialys right up to the very end—though at one point, remaining true to form, she complained, "You didn't get me chopped liver?"

I wish she'd told us! We make excellent chopped liver. It's not a traditional appetizing food, but even a place like Russ & Daughters has to change with the times.

GEFILTE FISH

Rae: Around the holidays I always think back to a children's book called *The Carp in the Bathtub*, about some kids who try to free a carp that was destined to become gefilte fish. The story is a throwback to another epoch—those who make this dish from scratch are so few and far between. Sure, you can get perfectly mediocre gefilte fish at a deli, or worse, in a jar at the supermarket, but making it at home gives you so much more control over its flavor, texture, and quality.

Carp, pike, and whitefish—all freshwater species that once thrived in the rivers and streams of Central and Eastern Europe—are the traditional fish for this classic Passover and Shabbos food, but finding fresh versions of these varieties can be hard. Whitefish and pike abound in the Great Lakes, but most fisheries smoke them before they hit the markets. And carp is often only available in Chinatown. If you can't find fresh versions of those three kinds of fish, fluke—or a combination of cod and salmon—are good alternatives.

The version we make at Mile End places the fresh, bracing flavor of the fish front and center. Despite its reputation for being rubbery and gross, good gefilte fish (*gefilte* just means "filled" or "stuffed" in Yiddish) is really just lovely fresh-ground fish with a few other ingredients to help bind it together. As per tradition, we serve our gefilte fish with chrain, the sharp and tangy beet-horseradish condiment.

2 pounds fresh boneless whitefish,
   pike, or fluke
1 medium onion, chopped
2 stalks of celery, chopped
2½ teaspoons Diamond Crystal kosher salt
1 teaspoon freshly ground white pepper
1 tablespoon sugar
3 large eggs
½ cup matzo meal

AFTER THE GRINDER:
¼ cup chopped fresh dill
1 cup minced carrot
1 cup chopped fresh chives
   Chrain (page 86), for serving

Cut half the fish into 1-inch chunks, place them in a large bowl, and thoroughly mix them with the onion, celery, salt, pepper, sugar, eggs, and matzo meal. Pass the mixture through the small plate of a meat grinder.

Cut the remaining fish into ¼-inch or smaller pieces and combine them with the ground fish, dill, carrot, and chives. Mix with your hands to incorporate.

Divide the fish mixture into 3 equal-size portions. Working with one portion at a time, transfer the fish mixture to a large sheet of plastic wrap. Form the mixture into a 6- to 8-inch cylinder and roll it very tightly in the plastic wrap. Place the wrapped cylinder onto another sheet of plastic wrap and roll it tightly a second time, twisting the ends as you go to force out any air and achieve a very tight cylinder. Repeat with one more sheet of plastic wrap. Then repeat the wrapping and rolling process with the remaining 2 portions of fish mixture.

Bring a large pot of water to a boil, reduce the heat to achieve a low simmer, and gently poach the 3 gefilte-fish rolls, in their plastic wrap, until an instant-read thermometer inserted into the center of a roll reads 155°F, 35 to 40 minutes. (You may need to weigh the rolls down with a heatproof plate or other heavy, heatproof object in order to keep them submerged.)

Transfer the cooked gefilte-fish rolls, in their plastic wrap, to the refrigerator until well chilled. To serve, unwrap the rolls and cut them into 2-inch-thick slices. Serve with the chrain.

SERVES 6 TO 8

Clockwise from top right: Lemon-Chile Pickled Asparagus, Pickled Fennel, Sour Pickles, Pickled Mushrooms, Pickled Beets, Pickled Peppers, Pickled Eggs

Pickles, Garnishes, Fillings & Condiments

VEGETABLE PICKLING BRINE

Noah: This is our mother brine. We use it for making our Sour Pickles (page 69), Pickled Fennel (page 72), Pickled Beets (page 72), and more. It's so versatile, and it can be stored at room temperature for months.

- ¾ cup plus 2 tablespoons Diamond Crystal kosher salt
- 10 tablespoons sugar
- 3 cups plus 4 cups water
- 3 cups cider vinegar (not "cider-flavored" vinegar)
- 3 ¾ cups distilled white vinegar

Combine the salt, sugar, and 3 cups of the water in a very large nonreactive pot, and warm the mixture over medium heat until the salt and sugar have completely dissolved and the liquid appears totally clear. Be sure to stir frequently to keep the sugar from burning on the bottom of the pot.

Add the cider vinegar, white vinegar, and the remaining water; stir. Allow the mixture to cool completely, then transfer it to containers, cover, and store at room temperature until needed. It will keep at room temperature for up to 2 months.

MAKES ABOUT 1½ GALLONS

QUICK CUCUMBER PICKLES

Rae: The miraculous thing about this preparation is that you can get that pickle-y sensation and flavor without having to put something in a jar and wait three weeks. In fact, it's quite the opposite: For this ultra-quick pickle, you've got to prepare it à la minute and eat it right away. Let it sit around and it'll get too salty. I think of it as I do a salad: something I make fresh right before serving the meal.

- 1 cup Diamond Crystal kosher salt
- ⅔ cup sugar
- 2 teaspoons freshly ground black pepper
- 4 teaspoons ground coriander
- 1 garlic clove, grated
- ½ English cucumber (about 8 ounces), skin on, sliced very thin, ideally on a mandoline

Mix the dry ingredients in a bowl. Toss the cucumber with 1 tablespoon plus 1 teaspoon of the spice mixture (save the rest; it will keep for months at room temperature). Let sit 10 minutes before serving.

MAKES 8 OUNCES OR 4 SERVINGS

PICKLED GREEN TOMATOES

Rae: Ah, the pickled green tomato, that stalwart of the pickle bowl at so many New York delis. At Mile End, we use ours as a garnish for our Veal Schnitzel (page 136), and we also fry them—so delicious—with a matzo-meal crust. You can use almost any size green tomato for this recipe: beefsteak, cherry, plum, and so on. It also happens to be the same basic recipe, with a minor tweak or two, as the one for our Sour Pickles (page 69).

1½ gallons green tomatoes, such as beefsteak, cherry, or plum (about 24 cups)

16 cups water

2 tablespoons plus 1 teaspoon Diamond Crystal kosher salt

2 or 3 dried árbol chiles (see Note, page 69)

3 fresh bay leaves

1 teaspoon yellow mustard seeds

1 tablespoon coriander seeds

5 tablespoons sugar

2 teaspoons black peppercorns

1 tablespoon dill seeds

8 garlic cloves, halved

1 bunch of dill

Vegetable Pickling Brine (opposite page)

Rinse the tomatoes and discard any damaged or bruised ones. In a large nonreactive pot or container, combine the water and salt and stir until the salt is dissolved. Place the tomatoes in a large nonreactive container, and add enough of the salt solution to cover them (discard any leftover solution). Allow the mixture to sit at room temperature overnight.

Rinse the tomatoes and transfer them to half-gallon mason jars or other large sealable nonreactive containers. How many you can fit in a single jar will depend on the size and shape of the tomatoes.

With a pair of kitchen scissors, cut the chiles and bay leaves into thirds and place them in a bowl with the mustard seeds, coriander seeds, sugar, peppercorns, and dill seeds. Stir to combine. Divide the spice mixture evenly among the jars of cucumbers. Do the same with the garlic cloves and the dill.

Pour enough of the vegetable pickling brine into each of the jars to completely cover the tomatoes, weighing them down with a heavy object if necessary in order to keep them submerged. (Reserve any unused pickling brine for another use.) Cover the jars tightly, and let the tomatoes marinate in the refrigerator for at least 2 weeks before using, turning the jars upside down (or stirring the containers) every 2 days to redistribute the pickling ingredients. The pickles will keep in the refrigerator for up to 6 months.

MAKES ABOUT 1½ GALLONS

PICKLED RED ONIONS

Rae: What could be prettier than pickled red onions? And tastier? Try them on the Smoked Mackerel Sandwich (page 131) or as a garnish for Chopped Liver (page 45). You can use the pickling solution to make the Pickled Belly Lox (page 57) as well.

- 2 cups distilled white vinegar
- 1 cup sugar
- 4 allspice berries
- 4 whole cloves
- ½ teaspoon yellow mustard seeds
- 1 teaspoon black peppercorns
- 2 fresh bay leaves
- 2 medium red onions, sliced into thin rings (about 2 cups)

Combine all the ingredients except the onions in a nonreactive pot and heat the mixture over medium heat, stirring occasionally, just until the sugar dissolves. Remove from the heat and let cool to room temperature (note: if you're using this recipe to make the Pickled Belly Lox, don't let the brine cool). Place the onions in a nonreactive bowl; set a sieve over the bowl and strain the brining liquid over the onions, discarding the spices (for the Pickled Belly Lox, you can skip the straining step). Allow the onions to marinate for at least 1 hour before serving. The leftover brining liquid can be refrigerated for up to 2 weeks and used twice more.

MAKES ABOUT 1½ CUPS

LEMON-CHILE PICKLED ASPARAGUS

Noah: In my book, a good pickle should have a bit of a kick. These pickles fit the bill; they're just a tiny bit spicy, with a bright, eye-opening bite. You can use them as a garnish for roasted chicken, in salads, or simply as part of a pickle arrangement.

- 1¼ cups cider vinegar
- 1 cup distilled white vinegar
- 2½ cups water
- 2 tablespoons sugar
- ⅓ cup Diamond Crystal kosher salt
- 4 garlic cloves, peeled
- 2 shallots, thinly sliced
  Zest of 3 lemons, in wide strips
- 30 black peppercorns
- 10 dried árbol chiles (see Note, page 69)
- 1 tablespoon coriander seeds
- 2 fresh bay leaves
- 3 pounds asparagus

Combine all the ingredients except the asparagus in a large nonreactive pot; heat the mixture over medium heat, stirring occasionally, just until the sugar and salt dissolve. Remove from the heat. Bring a separate pot of water to a boil; meanwhile, trim the tough base of the stems and any damaged parts from the asparagus.

Blanch the asparagus until crisp-tender, about 2 minutes for standard-size (1 minute for pencil-size; 4 to 5 minutes for jumbo), and transfer them directly to the brining solution. Let cool. Transfer the mixture to a nonreactive container, cover, and store in the refrigerator for at least 2 weeks before using. The pickles will keep in the refrigerator for up to 6 months.

MAKES ABOUT 3 POUNDS

PICKLED EGGS

Rae: These are super-easy to make and dress up all sorts of dishes. Set aside a couple of cups of the pickling juice from a batch of your Pickled Beets and you can make these eggs with almost no effort. The eggs are great as a garnish, but you can use them anywhere you'd use a hard-boiled egg—sandwiches, salads, or just on their own for breakfast.

6 large eggs
Juice from 1 recipe of Pickled Beets (about 2 cups; see page 72)

Boil the eggs for 8 minutes, refrigerate them until they're completely cooled, and then peel them. Add the peeled eggs to a sealable nonreactive container along with the beet-pickling juice. Refrigerate for 3 days, then remove the eggs from the brine. The eggs will keep, covered, in the refrigerator for another 3 days.

MAKES 6

PICKLED MUSHROOMS

Rae: On our trips to Israel, I always look forward to the roadside meals, and particularly to the oily mushrooms that start them. These silky, earthy-tasting mushrooms are really more akin to olives than to pickles. Since they don't have the salty kick of other pickles, they offer a nice contrast on a pickle plate, and they're a great side dish. We recommend using a good-quality extra-virgin olive oil.

1⅓ cups distilled white vinegar
½ cup sherry vinegar
¼ cup water
⅓ cup Diamond Crystal kosher salt
1 teaspoon black peppercorns
4 sprigs of thyme
2 sprigs of rosemary
2 garlic cloves, lightly smashed
2 pounds small button mushrooms, rinsed and patted dry
2 cups canola oil
1 cup extra-virgin olive oil

Combine the vinegars, water, salt, peppercorns, thyme, rosemary, and garlic in a medium nonreactive saucepan and bring to a boil. Remove from the heat. Place the mushrooms in a heatproof nonreactive container and pour the hot brining solution over them. Let the mixture sit at room temperature for 2 hours, stirring occasionally.

Drain the mushrooms and transfer them, along with the brining solids, to a sealable nonreactive container. (You can save the brining solution, refrigerated, and use it one more time if you like.) Add the oils, cover, and refrigerate for at least 2 days before using. The pickles will keep in the refrigerator for up to 2 months.

MAKES ABOUT 8 CUPS

SOUR PICKLES

Noah: When I was growing up, there was always a jar of pickles in the fridge. Instead of sticking our hand into a bag of potato chips, we'd stick it into the pickle jar. When I started dating Rae, she got into the same habit. We'd buy our pickles from Moishe's Steakhouse on Boulevard St. Laurent. They were labeled "kosher dill," but they were more garlicky than dill-driven. That's how we make our pickles at Mile End too.

25 kirby cucumbers	1 tablespoon coriander seeds
16 cups water	2 teaspoons black peppercorns
6 tablespoons Diamond Crystal kosher salt	1 tablespoon dill seeds
2 to 3 dried árbol chiles (see Note, below)	8 garlic cloves, halved
3 fresh bay leaves	1 bunch of dill
1 teaspoon yellow mustard seeds	Vegetable Pickling Brine (page 64)

Wash the cucumbers and remove any dried pieces of the flowers that may have remained on the base of the cucumbers. Discard damaged or bruised cucumbers.

In a large nonreactive pot or container, combine the water and salt and stir until the salt is dissolved. Place the cucumbers in a large nonreactive container and add enough of the salt solution to cover them (discard any leftover solution). Allow the mixture to sit at room temperature overnight.

Rinse the cucumbers and pack them snugly into half-gallon mason jars or other large nonreactive sealable containers. How many you can fit in a single jar will depend on the size and shape of the cucumbers.

With a pair of kitchen scissors, cut the chiles and bay leaves into thirds and place them in a bowl with the mustard seeds, coriander seeds, peppercorns, and dill seeds. Stir to combine. Divide the spice mixture evenly among the jars of cucumbers. Do the same with the garlic cloves and dill.

Pour enough of the vegetable pickling brine into each of the jars to completely cover the cucumbers, weighing them down with a heavy object if necessary in order to keep them submerged. (Reserve unused pickling brine for use in any of our other pickling recipes.) Cover the jars tightly and let the cucumbers marinate in the refrigerator for at least 2 weeks before using, turning the jars upside down (or stirring the containers) every 2 days to redistribute the pickling ingredients. The pickles will keep in the refrigerator for up to 8 weeks (only if left whole; they won't keep quite as well after being sliced).

NOTE: *You should be able to find árbol chiles in a specialty shop. If not, substitute 2 teaspoons of crushed red pepper.*

MAKES 25 PICKLES

Bob McClure
Co-founder, McClure's Pickles,
Brooklyn

Seven Things I Love About Pickles

1. They're a family affair.
My brother and I grew up pickling in Michigan with our mother and father. My mother learned pickling from her grandmother. And her grandmother grew up pickling with her own father and mother. Now I run the business with my brother, Joe, and my parents. I love being connected to a family tradition. It's something that I would probably do whether I had a pickle business or not. On any given summer weekend my wife, Natalie, and I will can a half-dozen jars of green tomatoes, or maybe try making our own pepperoncini. It's engaging with food and family in a way that I think is taken for granted today.

2. They change with the seasons.
In the last twenty or thirty years, consumers have become used to accepting that every kind of produce is available all the time. And we have to kind of be reconditioned to understand that if you want the best produce, that can't be the case. Pickling a cucumber or a tomato at its peak summer flavor is a great way to enjoy produce well after its peak season. I also love that our pickles vary in flavor throughout the year. For example, the pickles we make in the height of summer have fresh flowering dill in the jar, which gives a subtle fennel-like flavor. Flowering dill disappears as soon as summer's over. Its flavor gives you a connection to a very specific time of year. I cherish that.

3. They help you bond with your farmer.
If the vegetable or fruit is poor quality or past its prime, pickling isn't going to make it any better. You've got to use the absolute freshest, best-quality produce. Talking to a farmer will help you a lot in terms of navigating what vegetables and fruits are at their peak at what times of year. Also, you want to find a vendor who's selling produce that's been picked very recently, twenty-four to thirty-six hours before it gets to market—that usually means a local farmer.

4. They're the spice of life.
A lot of folks assume that my great-grandmother's original recipe was for traditional, nonspicy cucumber pickles—the tamer version of our product—but it was actually the spicy ones that we grew up making, the ones with the big red chile peppers thrown in the jar. That heat, for me, is just a beautiful thing.

5. They make everything taste better.
Every Christmas, my dad would chop up our pickled garlic, peppers, and cucumbers and put them into a hearty baked-egg dish that was just so much more delicious than your average frittata. And he would always put those chopped pickles on his turkey and chicken sandwiches. The spice from those pickles, with all those sweet-salty notes, adds such a nice layer of flavor to almost anything you're eating.

6. They're a science lesson in a jar.
A few years ago, when we were experimenting with pickling garlic in our Brooklyn lab, all the garlic in our first batch came out blue. I was dumbfounded. I thought, What are we going to do? I have all this expensive garlic. It took a lot of time, it took a lot of money. How am I going to sell it? What I didn't know then was that garlic has an enzyme that will cause it to turn blue if it comes into contact with aluminum or copper, which are both found in trace amounts in the water in this part of the East Coast. After that, we figured out that an easy way around the problem is to quick-pickle your garlic by blanching it in vinegar before you actually pickle it, to neutralize that enzyme. I love finding these things out. I love learning my way around a pH meter, or figuring out the ideal temperature for fermenting cabbage so it won't get slimy. I get so much pleasure from experimenting with all the properties of different vinegars, seeing what I can create.

7. Everyone loves them.
What did we do with all that blue garlic? We put little stickers on the jars that said, "Feeling blue? Eat it." And customers were like, "Ah, okay, cool," and they snapped them up. Something just clicks with people when you put food in a pickle jar.

PICKLED BEETS

Rae: We use these pickled beets as a garnish for our Pan-Seared Trout (page 148), but they'll pretty up all sorts of fish and meat dishes. For me, when it comes to that beautiful confluence of sweetness, tartness, and earthiness, nothing beats beets.

2 pounds red beets, peeled and cut into ½-inch pieces
2 teaspoons whole allspice berries
2 fresh bay leaves
6 sprigs of thyme
2 teaspoons black peppercorns
    Vegetable Pickling Brine (page 64)

Place the beets, allspice berries, bay leaves, thyme, and peppercorns in a nonreactive saucepan and add enough of the vegetable pickling brine to cover the ingredients by 1 inch. Bring to a simmer, cover, and cook over low heat until the beets are fork-tender, 30 to 45 minutes. Let the beets cool completely, then refrigerate overnight before using. Store in brine, covered, in the refrigerator for up to 6 months.

MAKES ABOUT 4 CUPS

PICKLED FENNEL

Noah: Fennel is pretty strong-tasting when raw, but when you pickle it, you give it a new dimension. What I love about this pickle, aside from the fact that it stays crunchy, is that you still get that distinctive, anise fennel flavor in the finished product. Fennel isn't a traditional Jewish pickle, but it should be the star of any pickle plate, as far as I'm concerned. Plus, fennel has a long season and is relatively cheap, and you get a lot of pickle from just a few fennel heads and not much labor.

2 to 3 medium fennel bulbs, trimmed of their stalks and any stringy outer layers
1 lemon
2 dried árbol chiles (see Note, page 69)
1 tablespoon fennel seeds
2 to 3 sprigs of thyme
    Vegetable Pickling Brine (page 64)

Halve each fennel bulb lengthwise, and cut each half into ⅛-inch slices. Place the sliced fennel in a 1-quart mason jar or other nonreactive container. Use a vegetable peeler to zest the lemon, removing the outermost peel (but not the white pith) in thin strips; add the zest to the jar. Halve the lemon and squeeze the juice into the jar. Then add the chiles, fennel seeds, and thyme.

Place about 3 cups of the vegetable pickling brine in a nonreactive saucepan and bring to a boil. Immediately pour the hot brine into the jar, reserving any unused brine for another use. Let the mixture cool. Cover and refrigerate for at least 2 days before using. The pickled fennel will keep in the refrigerator for up to 8 weeks.

MAKES ABOUT 8 CUPS

PICKLED CHERRY PEPPERS

Noah: Here's a pickle that packs some heat. We like to prepare these peppers whole, but I'd recommend slicing them open before using them and removing the seeds and pith, to tame the burn a bit. These taste great chopped up on a Chicken Salad Sandwich (page 125). If you can't find cherry peppers, you can use this same recipe for mild green chiles like banana peppers. You can even use bell peppers, but you'll want to add a dried árbol chile (see Note, page 69) or two to the pickling mixture to get that heat.

> 6 cups Vegetable Pickling Brine (page 64)
> 1 1-inch piece of fresh horseradish root
> 1 fresh bay leaf
> 6 sprigs of thyme
> 6 black peppercorns
> 2 sprigs of oregano
> 4 cups cherry peppers, halved

Bring the vegetable pickling brine to a boil in a large nonreactive saucepan. Meanwhile, add the horseradish root, bay leaf, thyme, peppercorns, and oregano to a sealable, heatproof nonreactive container. Then pour the hot brine over the dry ingredients. Stir to combine.

Add the cherry peppers to the hot pickling mixture. Use a plate or other heavy object to keep the peppers submerged. Cover and refrigerate for at least 2 weeks before using. The peppers will keep in the refrigerator for about 6 months.

MAKES 4 CUPS

CRANBERRY SAUCE

Rae: When we decided to smoke whole turkeys for Thanksgiving, it was a big hit. More than a few customers told us it was the best holiday bird they'd ever had. So it's a tradition now, as is our all-American—and not particularly Jewish—house-made cranberry sauce.

> 1 pound fresh cranberries
> 1 cup sugar
> 1 cup orange juice
> 1 cup water
> 1 cinnamon stick
> ½ teaspoon ground cloves
> ½ teaspoon Diamond Crystal kosher salt
> Zest of 1 orange

Combine all the ingredients in a nonreactive saucepan and bring to a boil. Reduce the heat and simmer for 20 minutes. Remove the pan from the heat and let it cool to room temperature. Remove and discard the cinnamon stick, then transfer half of the cooled mixture to the bowl of a food processor. Process until smooth. Transfer the smooth sauce to a sealable container along with the unprocessed portion of the sauce; stir to combine. Chill before serving. The sauce will keep in the refrigerator for up to 3 weeks.

MAKES 4 CUPS

RUSSIAN DRESSING

Rae: I'd never dare to put this on a smoked meat sandwich (though more than a few of our customers have asked us to do just that), but for corned beef, I've just got to have it—mayo, ketchup, and all.

> 1 **cup mayonnaise**
> ½ **cup ketchup**
> ½ **cup minced Lemon-Chile Pickled Asparagus (page 66) or Sour Pickles (page 69)**

In a medium bowl, mix all the ingredients together. The dressing will keep, covered, in the refrigerator for up to a week.

MAKES 2 CUPS

TARTAR SAUCE

Noah: We serve this sauce with our Smoked Mackerel Sandwich (page 131), but I think it's great on virtually any fish sandwich. You can use store-bought mayo instead of homemade if you like, but be sure to add a generous squeeze of lemon juice if you do.

> 2 **cups Lemon Mayonnaise (right)**
> 3 **tablespoons finely minced white onion**
> 1 **cup diced Lemon-Chile Pickled Asparagus (page 66)**
> 1 **tablespoon chopped fresh tarragon (optional)**

Place all the ingredients in a bowl and stir to combine.

MAKES 2½ CUPS

LEMON MAYONNAISE

Noah: Rae and I are not big mayo people—we believe mayo-based coleslaw is heresy, among other things—but this condiment is different: With the intense tanginess of preserved lemons, it doesn't have the cloying fattiness I usually associate with the ingredient. This is the stuff to use for Mile End's Chicken Salad (page 125), and as a base for our house Tartar Sauce (left). For a more traditional mayonnaise, just leave out the preserved lemon.

> 2 **wedges Preserved Lemon (opposite)**
> 2 **large egg yolks**
> ¼ **cup fresh lemon juice**
> 2 **tablespoons Dijon-style mustard**
> 1 **teaspoon Diamond Crystal kosher salt**
> ½ **teaspoon freshly ground white pepper**
> 2½ **cups canola oil**

Rinse the preserved-lemon wedges and remove any seeds, then coarsely chop them. Place the preserved lemon, egg yolks, lemon juice, mustard, salt, and pepper in the bowl of a food processor and process for about 1 minute. Continue processing while very slowly drizzling in the oil in a thin stream, ½ cup at a time. (Adding the oil too quickly will prevent the mixture from emulsifying.) Adjust the salt and pepper to taste. Store in the refrigerator for up to one week.

MAKES ABOUT 4 CUPS

PRESERVED LEMONS

Rae: Preserved lemons are a staple of Mediterranean cooking. I just love their tart, concentrated flavor and the way they perk up stews, hearty sautéed greens, roasted root vegetables, and meat dishes like our Veal Schnitzel (page 136). You'll need these lemons to make the Lemon Mayo, opposite.

- 12 lemons
- 1 cup Diamond Crystal kosher salt
- 1 fresh bay leaf
- 1 dried árbol chile (optional; see Note, page 69)
- 6 black peppercorns
- 1 sprig of thyme
- Juice of 12 additional lemons (about 3 cups)

Wash the lemons thoroughly and slice each one into 8 wedges. In a large bowl, combine the lemon wedges, salt, bay leaf, chile, peppercorns, and thyme; toss until the salt has thoroughly coated all the other ingredients. Let the mixture sit at room temperature for 4 to 6 hours, stirring occasionally to redistribute the salt. Transfer the mixture, along with any collected juice, to a 2-quart mason jar, packing the ingredients down firmly. Pour in the lemon juice until it covers the lemons.

Cover the jar and store it at room temperature, turning it over a few times every 2 to 3 days to redistribute the ingredients. Loosen and then retighten the lid after you do this in order to let any gases escape. After 2 to 4 weeks (depending in part on the temperature of your home) the preserved lemons will be ready to use: The rind should be soft, and the white pith should be translucent. At this point the lemons should be transferred to the refrigerator, where they will keep for 6 to 8 months.

MAKES ABOUT 8 CUPS

SALT SHALLOTS

Rae: I just love this garnish. These are flash-cured shallots, and they've got the same addictive salty-sweet thing going on as fried onion rings, but without all the frying and the fat. We put these on our trout entrée (page 148), and they're great on salads and sandwiches. You can use the same preparation with thinly sliced scallions, too.

2 to 3	large shallots, thinly sliced crosswise
1	teaspoon Diamond Crystal kosher salt
¼	teaspoon sugar

Mix the ingredients together in a small bowl, breaking apart any slices that are sticking together. Let the shallots sit for 15 minutes before using. They'll keep in the refrigerator for a day or two.

MAKES ABOUT ½ CUP

SCALLION SAUCE

Rae: We created this zesty, garlicky sauce for our Romanian Steak (page 139), but I think it works beautifully with all sorts of chicken and fish dishes. And it's so easy to whip up. Noah says he also likes it on steamed vegetables—though I can't remember the last time I saw him eat steamed vegetables.

1	bunch of scallions, roots removed
2	garlic cloves, peeled
¼	cup chopped fresh flat-leaf parsley
	Zest of 1 lemon
⅓	cup extra-virgin olive oil
½	cup canola oil
	Diamond Crystal kosher salt
	Fresh lemon juice

Bring a medium saucepan of water to a boil. Add the scallions and blanch them for about 30 seconds, until crisp-tender. Drain and plunge them into a bowl of ice water, then drain again. Chop the scallions.

Combine the scallions, garlic, parsley, and lemon zest in the bowl of a food processor and pulse several times. Then, with the processor running, add each of the oils in a slow, steady stream through the hole in the top; continue processing until the oils have emulsified and the sauce has a loose, fairly consistent texture. Add salt and lemon juice to taste.

MAKES 1½ TO 2 CUPS

GIZZARD CONFIT

Noah: So many people just throw away that little packet of gizzards that comes with a whole chicken. What a shame! The gizzards have such a rich, satisfying flavor, especially when preserved in fat in a confit. We call for gizzards confit in the Kasha recipe on page 158, but they also taste great subbed in for the chicken confit in the Spring Chicken (page 143).

- ½ **pound chicken gizzards**
- 1 **garlic clove, peeled**
- 1 **teaspoon Diamond Crystal kosher salt**
- ½ **teaspoon freshly ground black pepper**
- 1½ **cups Schmaltz (page 91) or duck fat, plus more as needed**

Preheat the oven to 225°F and place a rack in the center of the oven.

Combine the gizzards, garlic, salt, and pepper in a small, heavy-bottomed ovenproof pot or Dutch oven. Add the schmaltz or duck fat to the pot. There should be enough to cover the gizzards completely when the fat is melted; if not, add a little more. Bring to a simmer, cover the pot, then transfer to the oven. Cover and bake until the gizzards are tender but not browned, 2 to 3 hours. Let the gizzards and fat cool; refrigerate the gizzards in their fat until ready to use.

MAKES ½ CUP

CHICKEN CONFIT

Noah: We always confit the legs and thighs of the whole chickens we buy, and that rich meat, preserved in its own fat, gives so much flavor to main dishes like the Spring Chicken (page 143). The best part is that a confit like this one keeps for up to four weeks in the fridge, making it easy to pull out some of the meat for weeknight salads or pasta and grain dishes, including Kasha Varnishkes (page 158).

- 4 **whole chicken legs**
- 1 **tablespoon Diamond Crystal kosher salt**
- 4 **garlic cloves, peeled and cut in half**
- 2 **teaspoons black peppercorns**
- 1 **sprig of thyme**
- 1 **fresh bay leaf**
- 1 **sprig of rosemary**
  About 8 cups Schmaltz (page 91) or duck fat

Toss all the ingredients except the schmaltz or duck fat in a large bowl to combine thoroughly. Cover and refrigerate overnight.

Preheat the oven to 225°F. Rinse the chicken legs thoroughly and transfer them to a heavy-bottomed pot or Dutch oven. Add enough schmaltz or duck fat to cover the chicken pieces completely. Cook the chicken until the meat is nearly falling off the bone, about 2 hours.

When the chicken is cool enough to handle, remove it from the fat. Pull the meat from the bones and tear it into small chunks. Or, if not using it immediately, keep the meat intact in its fat and store it in the refrigerator for up to 4 weeks.

SERVES 4

CONCORD GRAPE JELLY

Rae: This tastes great on everything from challah toast to a plain old English muffin.

- 4 pounds concord grapes, rinsed and stemmed
- 6 cups sugar
- 1 cup water
- 10 green cardamom pods
  Zest of 2 oranges, in wide strips
  Zest of 6 lemons, in wide strips
- ½ cup freshly squeezed lemon juice, strained

Combine the grapes, sugar, and water in a nonreactive pot. Bring the mixture to a simmer over medium-high heat and cook, stirring often, until the grapes have broken down, 6 to 8 minutes. Place the cardamom pods and citrus-zest strips in a piece of cheesecloth and secure it with twine; add the cheesecloth bundle to the grape mixture. Cool to room temperature and transfer the pot to the refrigerator overnight. Meanwhile, place 4 to 6 spoons (regular dinner spoons are fine) in the freezer (you'll use these to test the jelly at the end).

Press the chilled grape mixture through a coarse mesh strainer. Discard the seeds. Return the strained grape mixture to a clean nonreactive pot, along with the lemon juice. Bring the mixture to a simmer over medium-high heat and cook until it begins to look shiny, 10 to 15 minutes.

TEST THE JELLY: Take one of the spoons from the freezer and place about ½ teaspoon of the grape mixture on it. Return the spoon to the freezer for 3 to 4 minutes. (Meanwhile, turn the heat to low and cover the pot so the mixture does not reduce further than necessary.) Remove the sample from the freezer and try spreading it; if it's not thick enough, uncover the pot, turn the heat back up to medium, and cook the grape mixture for another 5 minutes before testing a second sample using another frozen spoon. Continue this testing process until the jelly spreads smoothly. Let the jelly cool, then store it in the refrigerator.

MAKES ABOUT 6 CUPS

APPLESAUCE

Noah: I believe in unsweetened applesauce. Apples are naturally sweet already; you don't need to add more sugar. Doing so cancels out the nice tartness apples possess. That's why our applesauce just tastes like delicious, tart-sweet apples.

- 6 pounds apples, such as Braeburn, Fuji, or Cortland, washed, cored, and quartered (about 12 apples)
- ¼ cup fresh lemon juice, plus more to taste
- 1 cup water

Place all the ingredients in a large pot and cook over medium-low heat, stirring frequently, until the apples are soft, about 1 hour.

Let the apple mixture cool somewhat, then pass it through a food mill. Return the milled apples to the pot and simmer over medium-low heat until the applesauce reaches the desired consistency, and add more lemon juice to taste.

MAKES ABOUT 6 TO 8 CUPS

CIDER-MUSTARD GLAZE

Rae: For me, this is what takes our Smoked Mackerel Sandwich (page 131) over the top: The tangy, spicy-sweet notes just bring a whole new dimension to the dish. This glaze also works really well as a sauce for salmon. Make sure you've got real apple-cider vinegar—and not the stuff labeled "apple-cider flavored." It makes a big difference.

8 cups unfiltered apple cider
1 cup honey
¼ cup yellow mustard seeds
2 tablespoons brown or yellow mustard seeds
1 sprig of thyme
¼ cup apple-cider vinegar

Place all the ingredients in a large nonreactive pot and bring them to a boil over medium-high heat. Lower the heat to low and simmer until the mixture has reduced to 2 cups, about 2 hours. Remove and discard the thyme sprig and let the glaze cool. Store in a covered container in the refrigerator for up to 1 month.

MAKES 2 CUPS

MAPLE BAKED BEANS

Noah: At Mile End we serve these baked beans alongside our hot dog, but they're just as good *on* one—a variation of an old Quebec/Upstate New York specialty known, curiously, as the "Michigan dog."

1½ cups diced Lamb Bacon (page 52)
3 cups diced onion
1 pound white navy beans, soaked overnight and drained
5 cups chicken stock
2 teaspoons Diamond Crystal kosher salt
1 sprig of thyme
1 sprig of rosemary
1 fresh bay leaf
1 cup maple syrup
Freshly ground black pepper

Preheat the oven to 325°F.

In a heavy, ovenproof pot or Dutch oven, cook the bacon over medium heat, stirring frequently, until it just starts to brown. Add the onion and cook, stirring occasionally, until it's translucent. Then add the beans, chicken stock, salt, thyme, rosemary, and bay leaf and bring to a simmer.

Cover the pot and transfer to the oven. Bake until the beans are soft but not breaking apart, 1½ to 2 hours. Add the maple syrup and season with salt and pepper to taste; stir. Let the beans sit for at least 30 minutes—or, even better, in the refrigerator overnight—before serving. The beans will keep for up to a week in the refrigerator.

MAKES ABOUT 10 CUPS

SAUERKRAUT

Rae: Using natural fermentation to preserve foods is an age-old Jewish practice, and sauerkraut is one of the easiest naturally fermented pickles you can make: It takes nothing but cabbage and salt. You can find variations of fermented shredded cabbage in many parts of Europe, from the relatively quickly fermented kind you typically get with choucroute garnie in France to the longer-fermented tangy and translucent kind you'll find in Eastern Europe—a cousin of the cheap commercially made sauerkraut served with street-vendor hot dogs. The sauerkraut we make at Mile End is fermented just long enough to become tart and zingy, and it is absolutely delicious when served with our bratwursts and hot dogs.

Sauerkraut is traditionally fermented over a period of weeks or months in big glazed-earthenware crocks, but those can be expensive. Really, any large and clean food-safe plastic bucket—the kind pickles and feta are delivered to restaurants in—will work just fine; just ask a local restaurant or food store to save you a four- or five-gallon one, or order a couple from an online restaurant supplier. Some food-safe containers are made of clear plastic; if you use one of those, be sure to keep it out of the sun when fermenting, as sunlight can adversely affect the fermentation process.

Here's another tip: After you've earned your sauerkraut stripes with your first batch, you can speed up the process the next time around by adding a few cups of your last batch of sauerkraut, or just its liquid, to the new cabbage. By adding the live cultures from the finished product to a new batch, you can cut the fermentation time down to as little as seven days. For a similar shortcut, you can use some of the brine from naturally fermented pickles (the kind found in the refrigerated section of the grocery store, and not the shelf-stabilized pickles found in jars) to speed up the process.

5 pounds green cabbage (not Savoy)
   Diamond Crystal kosher salt

One 4- to 5-gallon earthenware crock
or food-safe plastic container

Remove the dark green leaves from the exterior of the cabbage. Quarter the heads lengthwise; cut out and discard the stem portion from each section. Shred the cabbage using the slicing disk of a food processor. (Or slice it as thinly as possible with a sharp knife.)

In a large bowl, toss the shredded cabbage with ¼ cup of salt, gently squeezing and massaging the cabbage to allow the salt to penetrate. Allow the cabbage to sit at room temperature for at least 2 hours or as long as overnight in order to allow the salt to dissolve completely and draw out water from the cabbage.

Transfer the cabbage, along with its accumulated liquid, to the earthenware or food-safe plastic container. Pack the cabbage as tightly as possible into the bottom of the container so that the liquid rises to the surface and the cabbage is submerged. If the cabbage is not fully submerged in its own liquid (this will most likely be the case), then make some extra brine by dissolving 3 tablespoons of salt in 8 cups of water. Add enough of the salt solution to cover the compressed cabbage by at least a half-inch.

Place a plate (one that fits the opening of the container as closely as possible) on top of the cabbage and weigh it down with something heavy, ideally a couple of clean zip-top bags filled with leftover salt solution (or some other liquid or solid that won't spoil).

Cover the container loosely with plastic wrap and store it in a cool, well-shaded place until the sauerkraut has a pleasingly sour taste and a very soft but noticeable effervescence on the tongue, roughly 3 weeks to 1 month (if stored at the ideal temperature of 60 to 70°F).

At this point the sauerkraut can be moved to smaller containers that can be easily stored in the refrigerator. Before repackaging, adjust the salt to taste; if you want to reduce the saltiness, just add more water. You can also add flavorings such as caraway seeds or mustard seeds if you like. The flavor of the sauerkraut will slowly intensify in the refrigerator over time. The sauerkraut will keep in the refrigerator for up to one year.

MAKES ABOUT 12 CUPS

EGG NOODLES

Noah: I first made these noodles for a kasha recipe I developed with the food writer Joan Nathan, who had asked me to come up with updated Hanukkah dishes for a *New York Times* article she was writing. (The kasha recipe appears on page 158.) I've always liked the bow-tie shape, but you can skip the pinching step if you want and still have a damn good noodle. One caveat: The noodles are pretty delicate, so you'll have to treat them more gently than you would store-bought dried noodles when you're tossing them with other ingredients.

2 **cups all-purpose flour (or 1 cup all-purpose flour and 1 cup durum flour), plus more for dusting**
2 **large eggs**
2 **large egg yolks**
 Water

Place the flour in the bowl of a food processor and add the eggs and yolks on top. Pulse until a dough forms. If necessary, add a tablespoon or two of water between pulses to help the dough come together. Transfer the dough to a floured surface and form it into a ball. Wrap the dough in plastic wrap and let it rest at room temperature for 1 hour.

Roll out the dough as thinly as possible on a well-floured surface (if you want to use a pasta machine, see steps 3 through 6): **1.** Shape the dough into a rectangle. **2.** Roll it flat with a rolling pin. **3-6.** Pass it through the machine with the rollers at the thickest setting, gently guiding it as it comes out of the rollers. Repeat, adjusting the roller setting, until the pasta sheet is as thin as possible. **7.** Trim off the rough edges. **8.** Fold the dough into thirds lengthwise, then unfold. **9-10.** Using the fold lines as a guide, cut the dough sheet into 2½-inch squares. **11-12.** Form the dough squares into bow ties by gently pinching them in the middle.

Let the noodles dry on a floured surface or baking sheet for 3 hours. If you're not cooking them immediately, let them dry fully overnight, then transfer them to large paper or plastic bags for storage in the pantry.

When you're ready to cook the noodles, bring a pot of salted water to a boil, add the noodles, and cook until tender, 3 to 5 minutes. Drain.

MAKES ABOUT 5 DOZEN NOODLES

MAKING EGG NOODLES

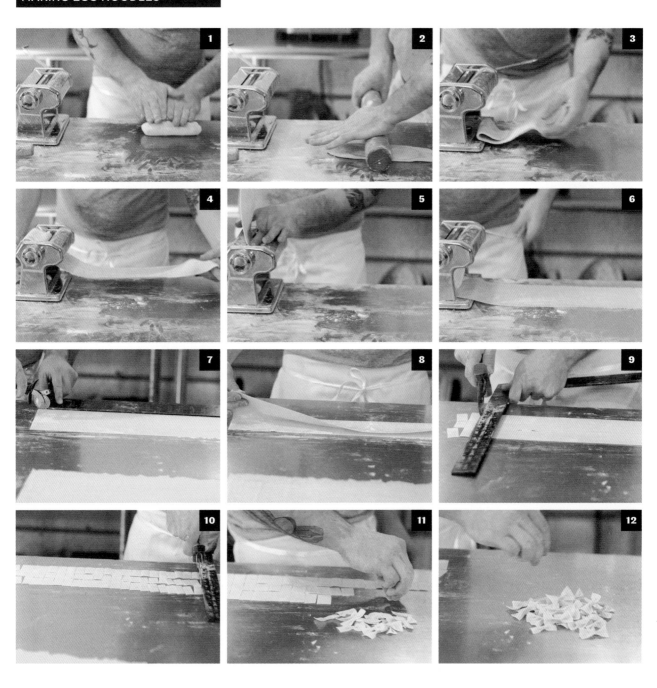

PICKLED HORSERADISH & CHRAIN

Noah: Anyone who's been to a proper Seder knows that raw horseradish is a gnarly, beautiful, sinus-clearing thing. My grandfather, not content to eat just the customary symbolic sliver of the proverbial bitter root at the Passover table, would eat a whole mouthful, so that he could cry real and copious tears for his exiled ancestors. Now, the key to turning the fresh root into a good condiment is to tame its sharp heat without obliterating it. Our pickled horseradish gets served with the Beef on Weck sandwich (page 128), and we also adapt that base preparation to make chrain, the bright-colored horseradish-and-beet condiment that's usually served with Gefilte Fish (page 60). Making chrain requires just a few added steps, which are shown below.

If you're really serious about horseradish, try growing your own. Our director of food operations, Michael Stokes, does: "Basically," he says, "you just take an unpeeled piece from the Seder plate and plant it in a large, deep flowerpot, with loose soil, just below the surface. Put it in a sunny spot and water it whenever the soil feels dry. By the next Passover it should be large enough to harvest."

1 large horseradish root (about 1 pound)
Diamond Crystal kosher salt
Distilled white vinegar

ADDITIONAL INGREDIENTS FOR THE CHRAIN:
1 large red beet, peeled and cut into 2-inch pieces
Sugar

Completely submerge the horseradish root in lukewarm water for about 30 minutes. Scrub the root with a vegetable brush under running water to remove all the dirt. (If the root is really crusted with soil, you may have to perform the above steps a second time.) Cut the root into 2-inch segments, and peel the pieces using a paring knife.

Pass the pieces through the fine-shredding disk of a food processor; transfer the shredded horseradish to a nonreactive container and push down on it gently to compact it. Add 1 teaspoon of salt and just enough vinegar to cover the shredded horseradish completely. Allow the horseradish mixture to sit uncovered overnight.

If you're making chrain, skip from here directly to the addendum below.

Drain the shredded horseradish, reserving the vinegar. Place the shredded horseradish in the bowl of the food processor and process for about 3 minutes, occasionally scraping down the sides of the bowl if necessary. While the processor is still running, slowly pour in 1 cup of the reserved vinegar. Continue processing for another 2 minutes.

Adjust the salt to taste. Add more vinegar if you would like a thinner mixture. If the horseradish is too pungent for your taste, just allow it to sit at room temperature overnight before using it. The horseradish will keep in the refrigerator for up to a year and a half.

TO MAKE CHRAIN: Once you've shredded the horseradish and set it out to rest, prepare the beets: Pass the beet pieces through the shredding disk of a food processor; transfer the shredded beet to a bowl and refrigerate them overnight.

Drain the shredded horseradish, reserving the vinegar. Place the shredded beet in a small nonreactive pot along with 1 tablespoon of sugar and enough of the reserved horseradish vinegar to cover the beet completely. Heat the pot over medium heat until the contents start to simmer; remove from the heat and let the beets cool.

Drain the beet, reserving the liquid. Place the cooked beet in the food processor along with the shredded horseradish and process for about 3 minutes, occasionally scraping down the sides of the bowl if necessary. While the processor is still running, slowly pour in 1 cup of the reserved beet-cooking liquid. Continue processing for another 2 minutes.

Adjust the salt and sugar to taste. Add more vinegar if you would like a thinner mixture. The chrain will keep in the refrigerator for up to 3 months.

MAKES A LITTLE MORE THAN 2 CUPS OF EACH

Jeffrey Yoskowitz
Writer, pickler, food entrepreneur & co-founder
of The Gefilteria, New York City

Exalted Peasant Fare

MY FATHER HAS ALWAYS SHIED AWAY from a prescribed Jewish life, avoiding Sabbath services and daily blessings, but it was always with piety and devotion that he worshipped tongue polonaise and other Eastern European Jewish fare. While my sisters and I sometimes joke that we mostly inherited our mother's physical traits, we all attribute the inexplicable pull toward chopped liver, latkes, and matzo ball soup to our father.

Yet we did not always eat these foods on a regular basis. Ashkenazi cuisine was relegated to major holidays, trips to my maternal grandparents' home, or the occasional jaunt into New York City from New Jersey when we paired dinner at the old Ratner's—usually blintzes and pickles—with a Broadway show.

Our father, who was the son of a nutrition-crazed vegetarian in the 1950s and '60s, grew up deprived of the Jewish comfort foods that made him happy. Grandma Lily, in an effort to cure her colitis, made her kitchen vegetarian and "healthy." Schmaltz was out. Same with babka. Even vacations to the Catskills were relocated to a local vegetarian hotel. To satisfy his cravings, my father had to sneak into Brooklyn streets to find solace in hot cherry-cheese knishes; he joined youth groups to eat frankfurters and cold cuts; he visited friends' houses to eat home-cooked chicken soup. It's no wonder that my father placed the traditional food of his ancestors in Poland on a pedestal. Eating Jewish was an expression of freedom for him. Eating old-world foods became an act of rebellion.

My sisters and I developed this shared adoration of traditional Eastern European foods. In a cruel twist of fate, my mother dealt with her own health issues as she reached middle age and converted our family to a healthy diet, replacing some of our cherished comfort foods with tofu and kale. I was reliving my father's trauma.

And so we ate our Jewish foods only on special occasions. I still associate vegetable kugel with Rosh Hashanah, potato with Passover, and gefilte fish and brisket with both holidays. Stuffed cabbage made its appearance on Yom Kippur, and blintzes were eaten hot and fresh when we visited Grandma Ruth in Swampscott, Massachusetts. Knishes were tasted only on my father's unsolicited nostalgic tours of old Brooklyn or at Manhattan delis.

For me, it wasn't the knish or the brisket that held such supreme pleasure and meaning but blintzes, specifically the sweet-cheese-and-cinnamon variety made by Grandma Ruth. When I first tasted them, I had never tried anything so perfect, nor eaten any food that was so deeply satisfying. They were not too sweet or gooey, more of a crepe than a fried pastry. When Grandma Ruth announced to my sisters and me when I was about twelve that she would never make her blintzes again, it came as a shock. "It is just too much work," she said, uttering the same phrase she had years prior when she stopped making gefilte fish and kreplach from scratch. It was the most jarring moment of my gastronomic memory. I grew nervous. What would we eat at Grandma's house? If they were not prepared by my grandmother or the local Jewish caterer, would we lose these Jewish classics?

Later, in my twenties, biding my time before heading to Israel, I worked at Adamah—a Jewish organic farm in northwest Connecticut. A bumper crop that season had left the farm with an inordinate number of cucumbers, and in a fit of inspiration, one of the young farmers suggested that they be transformed into pickles, following his grandmother's traditional recipe.

The utilitarianism of pickling and preserving resonated with what I came to understand as the clever and adaptive foundation of Jewish cooking. Pickles developed out of necessity and preservation, much like other peasant foods eaten by my ancestors. Knishes, for instance, were used to repackage and transport leftovers. Gefilte fish stretched how far one fish could feed a family. And cholent was made of the week's leftovers, sometimes from scrap meat, barley, potatoes, or whatever else was on hand, simmered together to be eaten hot on the Sabbath day.

With Hasidic-like zealotry, I now try to incorporate the building blocks of Eastern European cuisine into my daily living, be they pickles, schmaltz, or kasha. What makes traditional Jewish peasant food so special, whether eaten only a few times a year or on a daily basis, is not necessarily the rarity or the quality of the ingredients, but the cultural importance we bestow upon it. The real secret behind the best Jewish food, I have finally realized, is its humility and simplicity.

HORSERADISH CREAM

Rae: I like to think of this condiment as horseradish all dressed up—it's got hints of the root's eye-watering kick, but with a creamy, civilized veneer. We apply a slick of horseradish cream to the plate for our Pan-Seared Trout (page 148), and, really, it goes beautifully with all kinds of fish—especially on a canapé of Lox (page 56) and Pumpernickel (page 174).

> 2 tablespoons Pickled Horseradish (page 86)
> ¾ cup sour cream
> 1½ tablespoons extra-virgin olive oil
> ½ teaspoon Diamond Crystal kosher salt, plus more to taste
> Juice of 1 lemon

Carefully squeeze the horseradish over the sink to extract any excess liquid. Place the horseradish in a medium bowl with the remaining ingredients. Whisk the ingredients together vigorously; season with additional salt to taste if needed. The cream will keep in the refrigerator for up to 3 days.

MAKES ABOUT 1 CUP

SOUP MANDEL

Noah: These are the Jewish version of oyster crackers, and they're the classic accompaniment for Chicken Soup (page 151). This recipe will make a whole pound of soup mandel, but don't worry, they'll keep for weeks.

> 2 large eggs, beaten
> ⅓ cup Schmaltz (opposite page) or canola oil, at room temperature
> 2 tablespoons Diamond Crystal kosher salt
> ½ tablespoon freshly ground black pepper
> 1 cup water
> 4 cups all-purpose flour

Combine the eggs, schmaltz, salt, pepper, and water in the bowl of a stand mixer with a dough-hook attachment; mix on medium speed to bring the ingredients together, 5 to 10 seconds. Add the flour and mix on low speed until the dough comes together, about 5 minutes. On a lightly floured work surface, roll and knead the dough into a ball. Cover the dough ball in plastic wrap and let it sit in the refrigerator overnight.

Preheat the oven to 325°F. Take a golf ball–size piece of the dough and roll it into a very thin foot-long strip. Cut the strip into small pieces (each one about a quarter-inch long). Dust the dough pieces with flour and transfer them to a dry baking sheet. Repeat with the remaining dough.

Bake, rotating the tray 180 degrees halfway through cooking, until the soup mandel are golden and crisp, about 30 minutes. The mandel will keep, covered, in a cool, dry place for up to 1 month.

MAKES ABOUT 1 POUND

GRIBENES & SCHMALTZ

Noah: Gribenes—aka chicken skin cracklings—are a marvelous thing: They're like a hybrid of potato chips and bacon, but even better and cheaper. We use them to give crunch and saltiness to our Chicken Salad Sandwich (page 125) and our Chopped Liver (page 45). After we've made the gribenes, we just strain the rendered fat to make our schmaltz, which is another marvel owed to the resourcefulness of Jewish cooks. Schmaltz is a pure and lovely fat; you can use it in a warm vinaigrette, or spread it on challah before you toast the bread for a sandwich. At Mile End we also use it to enrich the stuffing for our Spring Chicken (page 143) and the filling for our Knishes (page 165). As if gribenes and schmaltz weren't miraculous enough, here's another sign that they're gifts from God: You can make both at the same time, and it can all be done in the oven. Call your butcher ahead of time to have him reserve the chicken skin and fat.

2   **pounds chicken skin with its fat**
    Diamond Crystal kosher salt

Spread the chicken skin and fat out on a baking sheet in an even layer. Place the tray in the freezer until the skin is partially frozen, about 1 hour. (This will make it easier to cut.) Transfer the chicken skin to a cutting board and cut it into 3-inch-long strips; then cut each strip crosswise into ½-inch pieces.

Preheat the oven to 350°F. Place the chicken skin pieces in a large roasting pan and toss them with 2 teaspoons of salt. Bake for 20 minutes, then remove the pan from the oven to give the skin pieces a stir. Return them to the oven and continue to bake, stirring every 10 minutes or so, until the chicken skin pieces have rendered their fat and are crisp and nicely browned. (The cooking should be monitored closely, especially as the chicken skin pieces start to brown, because they can go from browned to burned very quickly.) Remove the pan from the oven and let it cool for 15 minutes.

Carefully pour all the contents of the roasting pan through a metal strainer into a metal pot or other heatproof vessel. Leave the strainer over the pot to let the gribenes drain a couple of minutes more; then transfer the gribenes to a tray or plate lined with several layers of paper towels. Allow both the schmaltz and the gribenes to cool to room temperature.

Season the gribenes with more salt to taste if needed, and store them in an airtight container at room temperature for up to 3 days.

Transfer the schmaltz to a covered container and refrigerate it for up to 2 weeks.

TIP: *Schmaltz will keep well in the fridge, but the fresh factor is central to good gribenes. Make sure to eat all the cracklings within a few days.*

MAKES ABOUT 2 CUPS GRIBENES AND ABOUT 1 CUP SCHMALTZ

BEEF STOCK & BEEF JUS

Noah: This is the stock we use to make the jus for our Beef on Weck sandwich (page 128), among other things. It takes a day to make, but you can split the roasting and simmering process over two days if you prefer. It's packed with intense flavor, and you can freeze it for up to three months and use it as the base for all sorts of dishes and sauces, from French onion soup to almost any meat braise: brisket, pot roast, short ribs, whatever. One of the reasons it's so rich is that we use plenty of meat, and not just bones, to make it. As our own Michael Stokes told me once, "If you only use bones, you get a beef stock that tastes like bones." Mike also throws in a calf's foot, which is rich in collagen and gives even more depth to the broth. At the bottom of the recipe you'll find instructions for turning the stock into beef jus.

3	pounds beef stew meat, cut into 2-inch chunks
¼	cup tomato paste
1	pound beef bones, neck or marrow
1	calf's foot, cut into 3-inch sections by your butcher
2	medium onions, cut into 1-inch chunks
2	medium carrots, cut into 1-inch chunks
2	stalks of celery, cut into 1-inch chunks
2	heads of garlic, halved crosswise
10	black peppercorns
1	teaspoon Diamond Crystal kosher salt

3	sprigs of thyme
3	sprigs of parsley
2	fresh bay leaves

ADDITIONAL INGREDIENTS FOR THE BEEF JUS:

2	garlic cloves, peeled
2	fresh bay leaves
2 to 3	sprigs of rosemary
2 to 3	sprigs of thyme
	Diamond Crystal kosher salt

Preheat the oven to 375°F. Arrange the stew meat in a roasting pan in an even layer, place it in the oven, and cook, stirring occasionally, until nicely browned, 30 to 45 minutes. Transfer the stew meat to a large stockpot and set aside. Reserve the roasting pan and keep the oven hot.

In a large bowl, combine the tomato paste and ½ cup water; whisk together thoroughly. Add the beef bones and pieces of calf's foot to the bowl and toss until they're coated with the tomato-paste mixture. Transfer the bones and calf's foot to the roasting pan and cook in the oven, stirring occasionally, until browned, 45 to 60 minutes. Transfer the bones and calf's foot to the reserved stockpot with the stew meat, leaving any fat or drippings in the roasting pan.

Reduce the oven temperature to 350°F. Place the onions, carrots, celery, and garlic in the roasting pan with the fat and drippings; stir to coat. Cook the vegetables in the oven, stirring every 15 minutes or so, until they're roasted through and browned, about 45 minutes. Pour about 1 cup of water into the roasting pan and cook for another 10 minutes or so, to loosen any vegetables and burnt bits from the bottom of the pan. Transfer the roasted vegetables and any liquid to the stockpot.

Add the peppercorns, salt, and just enough water to cover the contents of the stockpot by 2 inches. Heat the stockpot over medium heat until the contents of the pot start to simmer. Adjust the heat to maintain a bare simmer and continue cooking, uncovered, skimming occasionally to remove any foam and fat that rises to the surface, for about 6 hours.

Remove the pot from the heat and add the thyme, parsley, and bay leaves. Allow the herbs to steep for 30 minutes; then, using a fine-mesh sieve or a colander lined with cheesecloth, strain the stock, discarding the solids (use tongs to remove the bones first if you want). Transfer the strained stock to sealable plastic containers and store it in the refrigerator for up to 5 days, or in the freezer for up to 3 months. Unless you've skimmed most of the fat while cooking, a firm, protective layer of fat will form when it's chilled; just leave it on there until you're ready to use it. Then cut around its edge with a knife and pop it off.

TO MAKE BEEF JUS: In a saucepan, combine 2 cups of the beef stock with the garlic, bay leaves, rosemary, and thyme. Bring to a boil, then remove from the heat; strain. Add salt to taste. The beef jus will keep in the refrigerator for up to 1 week, or in the freezer for up to 6 months.

MAKES ABOUT 12 CUPS STOCK, OR 2 CUPS OF JUS REDUCTION

Left to right: Apple Turnover,
Cinnamon Buns, Twice-Baked Challah

Breakfast & Brunch

THE BEAUTY

Noah: Home cooking is the foundation for a lot of what we do at Mile End, but we also owe a big debt to Montreal's Jewish restaurateurs. Of course there's Ruth Wilensky, the Montreal lunch-counter owner after whom we named one of our most popular sandwiches (see page 122), and there's also Hyman "Beauty" Skolnick, the almost-as-old proprietor of Beauty's Luncheonette, a seventy-year-old brunch spot at the edge of the city's Parc du Mont-Royal. Last time Rae and I were there, Hyman was still there, too, perched near the door, pointing us to our seats.

They serve a superlative bagel sandwich at Beauty's, so it seemed right to name our signature bagel special after them. The basic toppings—lox, cream cheese, tomato, and onion—are as familiar to a New Yorker as they are to a Montrealer. But our bagel is Montreal all the way: hand-rolled, parboiled in honey-sweetened water, dredged in sesame or poppy seeds, and finished in a wood-fired oven. They say Montreal bagels are like snowflakes: Every one is unique.

All of ours come from the legendary fifty-four-year-old wood-burning oven of Montreal's St-Viateur Bagels. Every time I eat one, it sends me back. There's nothing like eating a hot, chewy "white seed" from the top of the chute at 3 a.m. on a windswept Mile End sidewalk. That is bagel perfection. So is the Beauty.

> Cream cheese
> 1 bagel, split and toasted
> Lox (page 56)
> Sliced tomato
> Diamond Crystal kosher salt and freshly ground black pepper
> Thinly sliced red onion
> Capers

Spread some cream cheese onto one half of the bagel. Lay 2 or 3 thin slices of lox on top of the cream cheese, followed by 2 or 3 slices of tomato. Add a little salt and pepper to taste. Top it all off with 3 or 4 slices of red onion and a scattering of capers. Repeat with the other bagel half.

SERVES 1

THE MONT ROYAL

Rae: In a lot of Jewish households, latkes tend to be served only around Hanukkah, but I thought a good potato pancake deserved to be enjoyed more regularly at Mile End. And since fried potatoes in one form or another have always been essential to brunch menus—being such good hangover food—Noah and I decided to make the latke a foundation for a brunch special. Two lightly fried potato pancakes, nice and crunchy around the edges and soft in the middle, serve as the base; then come a few slices of lox and finally, at the summit, a dollop of cool crème fraîche and a sprinkling of minced chives. It's an elemental dish, and so we named it after Mont Royal, the hill in the middle of Montreal after which the city is named. After a long brunch shift, I've seen Noah swap the lox for smoked meat and, if he really needs some fortification, add a fried egg to the mix. I like the Mont Royal just the way it is.

  2 Latkes (page 168)
    Lox (page 56)
    Crème fraîche
    Finely chopped chives

Warm the latkes in the oven, then place them on a plate; lay 3 thin slices of lox on top of the latkes. Place a generous dollop of crème fraîche on top of the lox and sprinkle with chives.

SERVES 1

SMOKED MEAT HASH

Noah: This breakfast favorite has been on the Mile End menu since the very beginning. I noticed that when we sliced our smoked meat for sandwiches, we inevitably had trimmings and flaky ends left over on the cutting board that didn't look too good on a sandwich but were perfect for a hash. If you aren't making your own smoked meat, just use some leftover thick-cut pastrami or corned beef from your favorite deli or order ours online (see page 224). For me, the dish isn't complete without the two sunny-side-up eggs on top. Once in a while we get an order for the eggs to be done over hard, and Rae has been known to walk over to the table and gently persuade the customer of the glories of sunny-side up: the soft, runny yolk mingling with the savory hash. It's kind of what the dish is all about.

1½   **cups diced russet potato**
1   **small onion, finely chopped**
1   **cup Smoked Meat (page 33), broken into small chunks**
    Diamond Crystal kosher salt and freshly ground black pepper
2   **tablespoons canola oil**
2   **large eggs**
    Finely chopped fresh chives (optional)

Place the potato in a steamer basket and steam until tender but still firm, 8 to 12 minutes. Transfer to a bowl and add the onion and the smoked meat; stir to combine. Season with salt and pepper to taste.

Heat 1 tablespoon of the oil in a medium skillet over medium-high heat; add the hash mixture and cook, without stirring, for 1 to 2 minutes, until the bottom of the hash gets crisp. Use a spatula to turn the hash over; let it cook undisturbed until the other side starts to get crisp, another 1 to 2 minutes. Stir the hash and continue cooking, stirring occasionally, until it is well browned and crisp, 2 to 3 minutes. Transfer the hash to a plate.

Meanwhile, heat the remaining 1 tablespoon of oil in a small skillet over medium-high heat; crack the eggs into the skillet and cook until the yolks have just started to firm up around the edges but are still runny in the middle, 2 to 3 minutes. Carefully slide the sunny-side-up eggs onto the hash. Season with more salt, pepper, and chives, if you like.

SERVES 1 TO 2

THE DELI MAN'S BREAKFAST

Noah: This is our version of a hearty breakfast, and it's my favorite way to use our maple baked beans. We usually use our house-made duck and maple sausage with this dish, but you could also go with the veal and turkey breakfast sausage or just store-bought sausage—you can even sub in bacon if that's your thing. Rae makes her own version with salami. Whichever way you go, it's a festival of fat, starch, and protein that'll keep you going for the rest of the day.

2 links or patties Duck & Maple Sausage (page 44),
   Veal & Turkey Breakfast Sausage (opposite page), or store-bought sausage
½ cup Maple Baked Beans (page 81)
2 large eggs
   Diamond Crystal kosher salt and freshly ground black pepper
2 slices Challah (page 177) or other bread, toasted

Cook the sausage in a small skillet over medium-high heat, flipping once, until it's browned and cooked through, 5 to 6 minutes. Transfer it to a serving plate, leaving the fat in the skillet.

Meanwhile, warm the baked beans in a small saucepan over medium-low heat, stirring frequently to keep the beans from scalding.

Crack the eggs into the skillet and fry them, sunny-side up, until the yolks are just starting to firm up, 2 to 3 minutes. Season the eggs with salt and pepper to taste.

Lay the challah slices alongside the sausage on the plate. Spoon the beans on top of the challah, then lay the fried eggs over the beans and serve.

SERVES 1

VEAL & TURKEY BREAKFAST SAUSAGE

Noah: I've always liked the idea of a hamburger for breakfast, so at Mile End we call these kosher-style sausage patties "breakfast burgers." Veal turns out to be a great stand-in for pork in a recipe like this one, and since there's no messing around with casings and stuffing, you can make these sausages in no time the night before and just fry them up in the morning.

- 1 **pound each lean veal and turkey (or 2 pounds of one or the other)**
- ½ **pound veal breast**
- 2 **teaspoons Diamond Crystal kosher salt, plus more if needed**
- 1 **tablespoon (packed) light brown sugar or maple syrup**
- 2 **teaspoons freshly ground black pepper, plus more if needed**
- ¾ **teaspoon crushed red pepper**
- ½ **teaspoon ground nutmeg**
- 2 **teaspoons chopped fresh sage**
- 2 **teaspoons chopped fresh thyme**
- 5 **teaspoons chopped fresh rosemary**
  Canola oil

Cut the lean meats and the veal breast into 1-inch pieces, place in a large bowl, and add the remaining ingredients, excluding the oil. Toss well to coat. Cover and refrigerate the mixture for at least 3 hours or overnight.

Meanwhile, place your meat-grinding attachment in the freezer. When you're ready to grind, pass the meat mixture through the coarse die of the grinder.

Cook a small pinch of the ground-meat mixture in a pan or skillet with a drop of oil to test for seasoning. Adjust the salt and pepper as needed. Divide the ground-meat mixture into 8 portions and form them into patties. The patties can be refrigerated for up to 4 days or frozen for 2 months; when you're ready to eat, just heat a little oil (just enough to coat the pan or skillet) and cook the patties, flipping once, until they're browned and cooked through.

MAKES EIGHT 5-OUNCE PATTIES

Left: Smoked Whitefish; *Above:* Smoked Whitefish Salad

SMOKED WHITEFISH SALAD

Rae: It didn't take us long to figure out that, even in New York, it's hard to find fresh whitefish out of season, so Noah and I buy ours already smoked. Many big-city bagel shops and delis sell smoked whitefish, though often it's whole, which means it won't necessarily be flaked or deboned. We didn't want to mask the big, rich flavor of the smoked fish with lots of mayo, so we stick to lemon and olive oil, fresh dill, celery, red onions, scallions, and our lightly pickled asparagus—ingredients that bring all sorts of tangy, salty, bright flavors to the salad. We serve our whitefish salad with a toasted Montreal-style bagel, though it tastes just as good with hearty Rye or Pumpernickel (page 174) and even a little cream cheese.

1 smoked whitefish (2 to 3 pounds), skin and bones removed

12 to 15 spears Lemon-Chile Pickled Asparagus (page 66), finely diced

3 stalks of celery, finely chopped

1 small red onion, finely chopped

¼ cup chopped dill

5 scallions, finely chopped

Juice of 3 to 4 lemons

¾ tablespoon freshly ground black pepper

¼ cup extra-virgin olive oil

FOR SERVING:

1 bagel, split and toasted
Freshly ground black pepper
Finely chopped fresh chives
Extra-virgin olive oil
Lemon wedge

Combine all the salad ingredients in a large bowl and mix them together thoroughly with your hands. Add more lemon juice to taste, if needed.

To serve, place a heaping portion of the whitefish salad onto one half of the bagel, season with pepper to taste, sprinkle with the chives, and drizzle a little olive oil over it all. Serve with a lemon wedge.

MAKES ABOUT 6 CUPS

MISH-MASH

Noah: Like a lot of the dishes on the Mile End menu, the Mish-Mash wasn't our invention. Tony Koulakis—aka the Man of Grease—and his kids Nick and Nikki have been making heart-attack-inducing skillet breakfasts by the same name at Cosmo Diner in Montreal for decades. Their Mish-Mash has salami, chopped-up hot dog, bacon, ham, and four eggs. While we sub in fresh seasonal greens for most of the meat and some of the egg, the big difference between theirs and ours is that ours isn't sprinkled with the ash from Tony's cigarette. Of course, we also use our own rye bread and salami, which crisps up beautifully on the griddle and makes for an incredibly satisfying morning meal. We have a version made with our house-cured lox, which is very popular. Good-quality deli salami and lox will work fine with this dish if you don't have the time or inclination to make your own.

1 ½ tablespoons canola oil
½ medium onion, thinly sliced
   Diamond Crystal kosher salt
3 large eggs
   Freshly ground black pepper
½ cup Beef Salami (page 36), diced into ½-inch cubes
1 small handful arugula, watercress, or other fresh greens
   Toasted Rye (page 174), for serving

Heat the oil and onion in a medium skillet over medium heat, stirring occasionally, until the onion starts to soften; add a pinch or two of salt and continue to cook until the onion is nicely browned, 10 to 12 minutes.

Meanwhile, beat the eggs in a bowl and season them with salt and pepper to taste. Once the onion has browned, turn the heat up to high and add the salami to the skillet. Cook until the fat has rendered slightly and the salami crisps a bit around the edges, about 2 minutes. Then add the eggs and greens and cook, tossing and stirring the mixture frequently to break up the eggs and mix everything together. When the eggs have firmed up—about a minute—transfer the Mish-Mash to a plate and serve with toasted rye.

FOR A LOX MISH-MASH: Omit the salami, and after the onion has browned, add the beaten eggs, the greens, and ¼ cup Lox (page 56), cut into ½-inch chunks, to the skillet simultaneously; cook, tossing and stirring to mix everything together, for a minute or so.

SERVES 1

BLINTZES

Rae: The blintz is a classic old-world Jewish specialty, and a go-to food for Shavuot, when dairy dishes are traditionally served. We like ours with fruit compote, but anything from fresh fruit to sour cream to Applesauce (page 80) will work, especially with a drizzle of honey or a dusting of cinnamon sugar. You can even make a sauce by warming a cup of Concord Grape Jelly (page 80) together with ¼ cup water.

FOR THE CREPES:
- 4 large eggs
- 1½ cups whole milk
- ½ teaspoon Diamond Crystal kosher salt
- ½ teaspoon sugar
- ¼ cup rye flour
- ¾ cup all-purpose flour
- ¼ cup (½ stick) unsalted butter

FOR THE FILLING AND FOR FINISHING:
- 3 cups whole-milk ricotta, drained overnight in the refrigerator in a fine-mesh sieve lined with a double layer of cheesecloth
- 2 large egg yolks
- 1 teaspoon Diamond Crystal kosher salt
- Zest of 2 lemons
- 2 tablespoons unsalted butter
- Compote of your choice (page 193), for serving (optional)

MAKE THE CREPES: Combine the eggs, milk, salt, and sugar in a large bowl and whisk until the ingredients are incorporated.

In a separate bowl, mix together the two flours. Sift them into the liquid and whisk until the batter is smooth. Cover and rest the batter in the refrigerator for 1 hour.

Heat 2 teaspoons of the butter in an 8-inch nonstick skillet over medium heat. Pour in ¼ cup of the batter and swirl the pan gently to coat it. Cook until the edges of the crepe start to pull away from the pan, about 2 minutes. Then flip the crepe, cook it for a few seconds more, and transfer it to a plate. Repeat with the remaining butter and batter to make 6 crepes in all.

MAKE THE FILLING: Place the ricotta, egg yolks, salt, and lemon zest in a bowl and stir until thoroughly combined.

ASSEMBLE AND COOK THE BLINTZES: Working with 1 crepe at a time, spoon about ½ cup of the filling onto a crepe, fold in the edges of the crepe, and roll it up snugly around the filling like a burrito. Repeat with the remaining crepes and filling.

Working in two batches, heat half the butter in a large pan or skillet and cook 3 of the blintzes, flipping once, until lightly browned, 2 to 3 minutes. Repeat with the remaining butter and blintzes. Serve the blintzes with fruit compote.

MAKES 6

APPLE TURNOVERS

Rae: We developed these turnovers partly as a way to get more crisp fall apples into our repertoire—and also because I love pretty much any pastry made with fresh fruit. Here's the best part: The dough is the same as the one used for the rugelach, so if you make an extra batch you're already halfway there.

2 pounds firm, crisp apples, such as Braeburn or Granny Smith, peeled, cored, and cut into thin slices (about 4 apples)

2 tablespoons cornstarch

1 teaspoon ground cinnamon

½ cup (packed) light brown sugar
   Pinch of Diamond Crystal kosher salt

1 recipe Rugelach dough, chilled (refer to the "Make the Dough" section of the Rugelach recipe, page 209)

1 large egg, beaten, for the egg wash
   Coarse decorative sugar, for finishing

Combine the apples, cornstarch, cinnamon, brown sugar, and salt in a large bowl and let the mixture rest overnight in the refrigerator.

Press down firmly on the mixture in the bowl, and carefully pour out any excess liquid.

Line a 10-by-15-inch baking sheet with parchment paper and grease it with canola oil or cooking spray.

Divide the dough into 6 equal-size portions. Working with one portion at a time, shape the dough portion into a ball and flatten it a bit so it resembles a thick hamburger patty. Use a rolling pin to roll out the dough into a roughly 5-by-8-inch rectangle.

Spread about ½ cup of the apple filling along the long edge of the rectangle nearest to you and roll the dough into a tight cylinder. Trim ½ inch or so from the ends of the cylinder to square them off. Then use a sharp knife to lightly score the top of the turnover on the diagonal 3 times. Transfer the turnover to the prepared baking sheet. Repeat with the remaining dough and filling. Cover the turnovers with plastic wrap and refrigerate them for 30 minutes.

Preheat the oven to 350°F. Uncover the turnovers, brush them with egg wash, and sprinkle them with decorative sugar. Bake the turnovers for about 25 minutes, rotating the tray 180 degrees halfway through cooking, until golden brown.

MAKES 6

BAGELACH

Rae: Most often this breakfast pastry is called a cheese bagel, but I like the Yiddish name for this old-school delight, which is hard to find outside traditional Montreal Jewish communities. We've had Montrealers visit Mile End and freak out when they see we've got cheese bagels on the menu. This food isn't really like a bagel at all; it's a mildly sweet pastry filled with pot cheese—the curd of buttermilk—or some variation thereof. We use our own house-made whole-milk ricotta as the base for our filling, but cottage cheese works well, too. You can save time by starting with store-bought puff pastry, but choose one made with butter instead of shortening. Either way, they're just so satisfying, so good—especially with a little fruit Compote (page 193) on the side.

FOR THE FILLING:
- 1 pound whole-milk ricotta or cottage cheese, drained overnight in the refrigerator in a fine-mesh sieve lined with a double layer of cheesecloth
- 1 large egg, beaten
- ½ cup sugar
- ¼ cup all-purpose flour
- 1 tablespoon sour cream
- ½ teaspoon Diamond Crystal kosher salt
- Zest of 1 lemon
- 1 large egg, beaten, for the egg wash

FOR THE DOUGH:
- 1 recipe Rugelach dough (refer to the "Make the Dough" section of the Rugelach recipe, page 209)

MAKE THE FILLING: Combine all the filling ingredients except the egg for the egg wash in the bowl of a stand mixer fitted with the whisk attachment. Mix on medium speed until the mixture is smooth, about 3 minutes. Cover and refrigerate overnight.

SHAPE THE BAGELACH: Preheat the oven to 350°F and grease a 10-by-15-inch baking sheet with oil or cooking spray.

recipe continues →

Divide the pastry dough into 2 equal-size portions.
1. Working on a well-floured surface with one portion at a time, roll the dough into a roughly 14-by-7-inch rectangle. Trim off any irregular edges. **2.** Pipe about ½ cup of the filling in a straight line along one of the short edges of the rectangle. **3.** Brush a little egg wash along the base of the filling. **4.** Use a bench knife or pizza cutter to cut the egg-brushed lip away from the rest of the dough. **5.** Gently roll the edge of the dough around the filling so that the dough wraps over the egg-brushed lip to seal it, creating a cylinder. **6.** Bend the bagelach into a horseshoe shape.

Continue the filling-and-rolling process until you've used up the whole dough portion and have made 5 or 6 bagelach.

Transfer the bagelach to the prepared baking sheet, brush them with more of the egg wash, and bake for about 30 minutes, rotating the tray 180 degrees halfway through cooking, until golden brown.

MAKES 10 TO 12

HOW TO SHAPE A BAGELACH

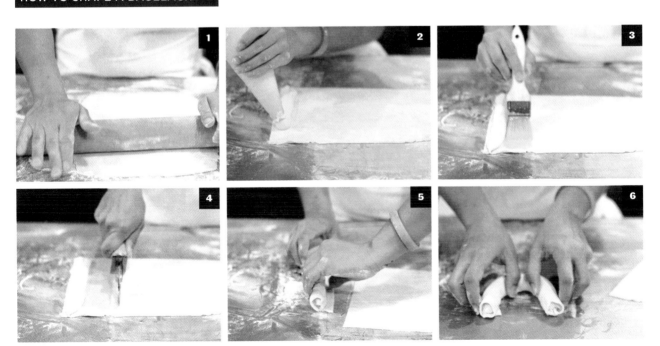

CINNAMON BUNS

Rae: These sweet buns are pure pleasure, and they're among my favorite things to serve at a Sunday brunch, especially if I've made challah the Friday before. I just make an extra batch of the dough and set it aside for the cinnamon buns.

FOR THE FILLING:
- ½ cup maple syrup
- 1 cup (2 sticks) unsalted butter, at room temperature
- 1 cup (packed) light or dark brown sugar
- ½ cup sugar
- ½ cup all-purpose flour
- 1 tablespoon Diamond Crystal kosher salt
- 2 tablespoons ground cinnamon
- 1 cup pecan pieces

- 1 recipe Challah dough (follow the Challah recipe on page 177 through to the end of the "Make the Dough" section)
- 1 large egg, beaten, for the egg wash

FOR THE FROSTING:
- 2 cups powdered sugar
- ½ cup half-and-half
- 1 teaspoon vanilla extract

MAKE THE FILLING: Combine the filling ingredients in the bowl of a food processor and process until the mixture is a smooth, thick paste, 3 to 4 minutes.

SHAPE AND BAKE THE BUNS: Line a 10-by-15-inch baking sheet with parchment paper and grease it with oil or cooking spray.

On a well-floured surface, press and stretch the challah dough into a large rectangle roughly the size of the baking sheet. Arrange the rectangle with the long edge closest to you, and spread the filling evenly over the surface of the dough, leaving a roughly 2-inch strip of dough uncovered at the far edge of the rectangle. Starting with the edge closest to you, roll the dough into a tight cylinder, stopping just before you reach the uncovered far edge. Brush the exposed lip of dough with the egg wash and then finish rolling the cylinder.

Slice the cylinder into roughly 2-fingers-wide buns, and transfer the buns to the prepared baking sheet, placing them close to one another but just shy of touching.

Cover the sheet with plastic wrap and let the buns rest in a warm, draft-free area until roughly doubled in size, about 1 hour.

Preheat the oven to 350°F. Bake the buns for about 15 minutes, rotating the tray 180 degrees halfway through cooking, until golden brown on top.

MAKE THE FROSTING: While the rolls are cooling, make the frosting by stirring together the powdered sugar, half-and-half, and vanilla in a medium bowl. Once the buns have cooled to room temperature, use a spoon to drizzle the frosting over them.

MAKES 6 TO 8

TWICE-BAKED CHALLAH

Noah: Like so many delicious foods, this challah was born of thrift and necessity. We found that on any given morning we had plenty of leftover challah, but not enough room on our griddle to make French toast with it. So we took a cue from the French boulangerie tradition of using day-old brioche for a sweet pastry and came up with a rich syrup and topping for the bread that would take well to baking. We like to serve it with fruit Compote (page 193). (Note: You can make the topping ahead and refrigerate it for up to five days; the syrup will keep in the refrigerator for up to a week.)

FOR THE SYRUP:
- ½ cup sugar
- 1 cup water
- ½ cup orange juice
- ½ tablespoon vanilla extract
- 1 cup maple syrup, plus more for serving

FOR THE TOPPING:
- ½ cup (1 stick) unsalted butter, at room temperature
- ½ pound almond paste, broken into pieces
- ½ cup slivered almonds, plus more for garnish
- ¼ teaspoon almond extract
- 2 large eggs, at room temperature
- ½ cup all-purpose flour
- 1 cup dried cherries

- 8 1-inch-thick slices of stale Challah (page 177), preferably day-old or older

MAKE THE SYRUP: Combine the sugar, water, orange juice, vanilla, and maple syrup in a medium saucepan and bring to a boil, stirring occasionally. Remove the pan from the heat and let cool; set the syrup mixture aside.

MAKE THE TOPPING: Put the butter in the bowl of a stand mixer and, using the paddle attachment, mix on medium speed for a few seconds. Add the almond paste and mix on low speed for a few seconds, scraping down the sides of the bowl. Mix on medium speed until the mixture comes together, about 1 minute. Add the sliced almonds and mix on medium speed for 20 to 30 seconds, stopping to scrape down the bowl if necessary. While the mixer is still running, add the almond extract and mix until it's incorporated, a few seconds more.

In a separate bowl, beat the eggs and then restart the mixer at medium speed. While the mixer is running, slowly pour in the eggs; continue mixing until they're fully incorporated, about 30 seconds. Add the flour and mix on low speed for about 30 seconds more. Add the dried cherries and use a spatula to fold them in by hand.

ASSEMBLE AND BAKE THE CHALLAH: Preheat the oven to 350°F and line a 10-by-15-inch baking sheet with parchment or grease it with canola oil or cooking spray.

Quickly dunk the slices of challah into the syrup mixture, shake off any excess, and lay them on the prepared baking sheet. Spread about ½ cup of the topping onto each slice of challah, distributing it all the way to the edges of the bread. Sprinkle with slivered almonds.

Bake the challah, rotating the tray 180 degrees halfway through cooking, until golden brown, about 20 minutes. Serve either warm or at room temperature, and for extra sweetness drizzle some maple syrup over the challah before serving.

TIP: *It's important to use stale bread; it should be crisp to the touch. You can even slice the challah and leave it out to dry overnight.*

SERVES 4

Corned Beef Sandwich

Sandwiches & Salads

SMOKED MEAT SANDWICH

Noah: What constitutes the "perfect" Montreal-style smoked meat sandwich is a matter of taste. Of course you've got to have good-quality meat that's smoked, steamed, and sliced on the premises, but that's never really called into question. Nor are the accompaniments, which almost invariably consist of two slices of rye bread and some mustard. The subtleties lie in the fat, or absence thereof. Many Montrealers consider the ideal smoked meat sandwich to be one that contains 50 percent first-cut or flat (meat from the leaner portion of the brisket) and 50 percent deckle (from the smaller, fattier portion). Others like a leaner 80-20 split. The truly ascetic will ask for an ultra-lean "100 percent first-cut" sandwich, whereas the truly decadent (count me among them) may go for 80 or even 90 percent deckle. Your prerogative, your pleasure. One other thing: Unlike many a New York pastrami bomb, a good smoked meat sandwich shouldn't be a foot-high tower of meat. You should be able to get your mouth around it, and it should satisfy but not overwhelm.

  Brown mustard
2 slices Rye Bread (page 174)
7 ounces Smoked Meat (page 33), steamed and sliced
  ¼ inch thick (see instructions on page 23)

Spread mustard on one slice of bread. Then start building the sandwich by laying 4 or 5 slices of smoked meat, each slightly overlapping the other, shingle-style, on the bottom dry piece of bread. Then arrange a second layer of 4 or 5 overlapping slices on top of the first. (Try to alternate layers from the first-cut or flat with layers from the deckle.) Top with the remaining piece of bread.

SERVES 1

THE RUTH WILENSKY

Noah: No establishment calling itself a Montreal-style deli should be allowed to do business without paying homage to Ruth Wilensky, the ninety-plus-year-old proprietor of Wilensky's Light Lunch. She's presided over that fabled lunch counter in Montreal's Mile End neighborhood since 1932, and the mainstay of the menu has always been the Special: a hot pressed salami sandwich served on an onion roll (which Ruth bills as pletzel; see page 184) with yellow mustard. When Ruth heard that someone had opened a deli in New York City called Mile End and had christened a salami sandwich in her name, she is said to have responded, "Well, you've still got to come to Montreal for the original." I can't argue with that.

Our version of the "Special" features two of Mile End's best products: our smoked salami and our made-daily onion rolls. We fry the thinly sliced salami for a few minutes so that it gets crisp around the edges and the fat starts to render, making for a little blockbuster of a sandwich: compact, intense, meaty. The more formidable Smoked Meat Sandwich (page 121) is still the main attraction at Mile End, but the Ruth Wilensky is the unsung hero of our lunch menu.

> 10 thin slices Beef Salami (page 36)
>   Brown mustard
>   1 Onion Roll (page 182), split

Place a skillet over medium-high heat and arrange the salami slices in 2 overlapping rows of 5 slices each, with each slice overlapping the other, shingle style. (This will allow you to flip all the salami slices at once in the skillet.) Cook until the fat starts to render and the salami starts to get crisp around the edges, 2 to 3 minutes. Flip the salami and cook for another minute or two.

Meanwhile, spread some mustard on both halves of the onion roll. Place the hot salami onto one of the halves of the roll; top with the other half. Transfer the sandwich to the skillet over medium heat and press down on it firmly with a steak weight or metal spatula; cook for 2 to 3 minutes, flip the sandwich, and cook for another minute. Transfer to a plate.

TIP: *Before you put them in the skillet, stack your slices of salami and make 2 or 3 small incisions in the outside edge to prevent cupping when cooking.*

SERVES 1

CHICKEN SALAD SANDWICH

Rae: Mile End's chicken salad is very good. But for me, what really makes this sandwich sing is the accompaniments. Since the salad itself is mayo-based and pretty creamy, we sprinkle on some of our house-made gribenes—chicken-skin cracklings—to give a burst of salt and crunchiness. Then we add a sweet-hot-sour kick with our pickled cherry peppers, and finish with our refreshing quick cucumber pickles. Finally, onto the thick-cut challah goes a schmear of schmaltz to bring it all together. If you really want to go wild, toast the challah schmaltz-side down in a skillet before putting the sandwich together.

FOR THE CHICKEN SALAD:
- 1 whole chicken, approximately 3 pounds
  Diamond Crystal kosher salt
- 4 scallions, finely chopped
- 3 stalks of celery, finely chopped
- 1 cup Lemon Mayonnaise (page 74) or store-bought mayonnaise
  Freshly ground black pepper

FOR THE SANDWICH:
Schmaltz (page 91)
Slices of Challah (page 177)
Gribenes (page 91)
Quick Cucumber Pickles (page 64)
Pickled Cherry Peppers (page 73)

MAKE THE CHICKEN SALAD: Place the chicken in a large pot of salted water and bring to a boil; reduce the heat and cook at a steady simmer until cooked through, about 1 hour. Remove the chicken from the pot and let cool completely. Remove the skin (discard it or reserve it for another use) and pull the meat off the bones. Coarsely shred the meat.

Place the shredded chicken in a large bowl and add the scallions, celery, and mayonnaise. Mix the ingredients together with your hands until they're thoroughly combined. Season with salt and pepper to taste; stir to combine.

TO ASSEMBLE ONE SANDWICH: Spread some of the schmaltz onto a single side of 2 slices of challah, and place the slices schmaltz-side down onto a dry skillet over medium-high heat. Once the bread slices are lightly toasted around the edges, transfer them to a plate, schmaltz-side up. To one of the slices add a generous scoop of the chicken salad (at the deli we pile it pretty high) and top it with some gribenes, cucumber pickles, and cherry peppers. Place the second slice on top and press down gently.

TIP: *If you make the Chicken Soup (page 151), you can use that meat and skip the first step.*

MAKES ABOUT 4 CUPS OF CHICKEN SALAD (6 SANDWICHES' WORTH)

Ken Gordon
Owner, Kenny and Zuke's Delicatessen,
Portland, Oregon

An Ode to Pastrami

IT ALL BEGAN FOR ME WITH a simple declarative statement on a local food blog: "There's no good pastrami in Portland." Then the challenge: "Ken does BBQ—he should try to make some good pastrami!"

From those few simple words sprang a deli that for the past four years has produced and sold almost a half million pounds of the famous smoked, spiced beef, with plans in the works to start wholesaling and doubling that output.

What is it about pastrami that fuels meat lovers' passions so? That no matter what city aficionados find themselves in, a search is made for the "real stuff" or "meat crack," as my wife, Leslee, puts it.

I'm often asked by neophytes what the difference is between corned beef and pastrami. The analogy I sometimes use is the difference between chopped liver and foie gras—both are liver, and not that there's anything wrong with chopped liver, but . . .

Don't get me wrong—I love a good corned beef on rye. But pastrami . . . there's something that happens . . . something alchemical and otherworldly when a piece of beef is subjected to the spicing, smoking, and steaming that we put it through to make pastrami. We lose about 40 percent in shrinkage by the time it gets onto the plate, but it's as if the flavor from that 40 percent melted into the other 60. And then some. The result is almost too salty, but not. And almost too intense, but just short. I've had vegans cross the line for one of my sandwiches (which I consider a blow struck for carnivores everywhere!). Pastrami deserves another category beyond simply "meat."

I remember growing up in Queens, New York, when Jewish delis were our go-to place for neighborhood dinners out—this was before every neighborhood had three Thai, two Burmese, two French, and three Italian restaurants, each concentrating on the food of a region you've never heard of. The deli man was back there behind the counter, trimming and slicing his giant mounds of pastrami and corned beef, offering tastes and crusty bits to whoever was in range, exchanging knowing nods with each. He was a god, and he assembled my favorite—pastrami, corned beef, chopped liver, coleslaw, and Russian on rye. It was as big as my head, and my jaw used to hurt trying to fit my mouth around it. But oh my, it was tasty! This sandwich is now known as the Ken's Special at Kenny and Zuke's.

There used to be thousands of Jewish delis in New York City. Now there are a couple of dozen. Dietary changes, economics, and uniformity of product have been the common enemies. But I still remember the flavor of that pastrami I ate as a kid, the intensity and spiciness and mouthfeel, with a perfect mix of lean and fat. That's what I've tried to duplicate, though I fret about ever getting it just right, so idealized is the original. Gotta keep trying, though.

There's something about watching people eat. I think it's one of the things that drew me to becoming a chef. Before that first bite there's an expectation, mixed with a yearning, a small dose of doubt and wariness: "Will this taste as good as I want it to?" After that first taste, the look changes—sometimes relief, sometimes disappointment, at times delight.

When I place a pastrami sandwich in front of a first-time customer, I watch carefully. There's the look, as in "Really, pastrami in Portland, Oregon?" There's the bite. The pause. Then the smile. Ah, pastrami . . . makes my job easy!

BEEF ON WECK

Rae: When I was first getting to know Rich Maggi, Mile End's baker, he would always rhapsodize to me about a sandwich called beef on weck, a specialty of Buffalo, New York, not too far from where he grew up (and roughly equidistant, as it happens, from Brooklyn and Montreal). "Weck" is short for *Kummelweck*, which is German for "caraway roll," Rich explained, and Buffalo-style weck is topped not just with caraway seeds but also plenty of coarse salt, making for a terrifically flavorful sandwich platform (see page 182 for the recipe). So when our meat supplier mentioned that she could get us some really excellent wagyu beef chuck-eye roll—perfect for roasting—we decided to start making our own weck and put Rich's favorite sandwich on the menu. Our version stands entirely on the quality of its ingredients: thin-sliced medium-rare roast beef, savory beef jus, a fresh house-made weck roll dunked in the jus, and Mile End's own horseradish. This is one tangy, meaty roast-beef sandwich.

¼ cup Beef Jus (page 92)
5 ounces thin-sliced Roast Beef (page 41)
   Pickled Horseradish (page 86)
1 Weck Roll (page 182), split and lightly toasted

In a medium saucepan over medium heat, bring the jus to a simmer. With a pair of tongs, put the beef in the broth and cook it for 1 to 2 minutes, until warmed through. Spread horseradish on the bottom half of the weck roll, remove the beef from the jus, and place it atop the horseradish. Dip the top half of the roll several times in the beef jus and place it on top of the roast beef.

SERVES 1

THE GRANDPA

Noah: A turkey sandwich is a safe harbor for customers who aren't quite ready to commit themselves to the glories of smoked meat, corned beef, or salami. We make our turkey sandwich with super-moist brined and smoked turkey breast, served on house-made rye bread with mustard—there's nothing to it, except great ingredients.

7 ounces Smoked Turkey breast (page 50), hand-sliced
2 slices Rye Bread (page 174)
Spicy brown mustard, such as Gulden's

Use a basket steamer to steam the sliced turkey until it's very moist and tender, 2 to 3 minutes. Serve on the rye with the mustard.

SERVES 1

CORNED BEEF SANDWICH

Rae: We run a Jewish deli in Brooklyn, so we just could not in good conscience omit this most classic of New York deli sandwiches from our repertoire. This one is by-the-book and delicious: just flaky, tender corned beef piled on fresh pumpernickel with tart vinegar coleslaw and our house-made Russian dressing. Note: This recipe is for a hot sandwich, but you can make a cold version if you want; just skip the steaming step.

7 ounces sliced Corned Beef (page 39)
Russian Dressing (page 74)
2 slices Pumpernickel Bread (page 174), lightly toasted
½ cup Coleslaw (page 133)

Steam the corned beef until very tender, about 5 minutes. Spread the Russian dressing generously on each slice of bread. Pile the corned beef on the bottom slice; top with the coleslaw and remaining slice of bread.

SERVES 1

SMOKED MACKEREL SANDWICH

Rae: I'm crazy about this sandwich. For one thing, it's healthy. For another, it tastes incredibly fresh, unlike so many fish sandwiches. Plus, it's a great way to use our house-made smoked mackerel. The crunchy watercress, tangy cider-mustard glaze, pickled red onions, and tartar sauce magically brighten up those traditional Jewish smoked-fish flavors.

1	4-ounce piece of Smoked Mackerel (page 53)
3	tablespoons Cider-Mustard Glaze (page 81)
2 or 3	sprigs of watercress, rinsed and dried
½	teaspoon fresh lemon juice
1	teaspoon extra-virgin olive oil
	Pinch of Diamond Crystal kosher salt
1	tablespoon Tartar Sauce (page 74)
1	Kaiser Roll (page 182), split and toasted
1	tablespoon Pickled Red Onions (page 66)

Preheat the oven to 375°F. Place the mackerel in an oven-safe dish and spread the cider-mustard glaze over the top. Bake the mackerel until heated through, 8 to 10 minutes.

Meanwhile, in a small bowl, toss the watercress with the lemon juice, olive oil, and salt. Spread the tartar sauce on the bottom half of the kaiser roll and place the mackerel on top. Top with the pickled onions, watercress, and the top half of the roll.

TIP: *Don't cut the sandwich in half; the fish will fall apart.*

SERVES 1

POTATO SALAD

Noah: This is the Zelig of potato salads—it can turn up anywhere and fit in just fine. It's as good on the dinner table served with schnitzel as it is at a picnic. The dressing is tart and super-savory, sparkling with lemon juice and spicy brown mustard, which mingle so beautifully with the flavors of scallions, red onion, and parsley.

FOR THE DRESSING:

- 2 large egg yolks
- 2 tablespoons spicy brown mustard, such as Gulden's
  Juice of 1 lemon
- 2 tablespoons white wine vinegar
- 1 ¼ teaspoons Diamond Crystal kosher salt
- 3 garlic cloves, peeled
- 1 ¾ cups canola oil

FOR THE SALAD:

- 3 pounds small red potatoes
  Diamond Crystal kosher salt
- 2 tablespoons extra-virgin olive oil
- 6 scallions, roots trimmed off
- ⅔ cup chopped fresh flat-leaf parsley leaves and stems
- 1 cup thinly sliced red onion
  Freshly ground black pepper

MAKE THE DRESSING: Combine all the dressing ingredients except the oil in the bowl of a food processor. Process until smooth and roughly tripled in volume, about 3 minutes. Then, with the processor running, add the oil in a slow, steady stream through the hole in the top; continue processing until the oil is fully emulsified. Set the dressing aside.

MAKE THE SALAD: Place the potatoes in a large pot and add enough water to cover them by 2 inches; add about ½ cup of salt and bring to a boil. Lower the heat and simmer until a knife inserted into one of the potatoes meets no resistance, 15 to 20 minutes. Drain the potatoes and, when they're cool enough to handle, quarter them; then let them cool completely.

Heat the oil in a pan or skillet over high heat. Cut the scallions in half crosswise and add them to the pan with a generous pinch of salt. Cook the scallions, turning them once or twice, until they're lightly charred, 3 to 4 minutes. Transfer the scallions to a cutting board and chop them into 1-inch pieces.

Combine the scallions, potatoes, parsley, and red onion in a large bowl. Add about 2 cups of the dressing to the bowl and mix vigorously with a wooden spoon until the dressing has been thoroughly incorporated and the potatoes have broken up a bit. Season with salt and pepper to taste. The potato salad will keep in the refrigerator for up to 3 days.

MAKES ABOUT 10 CUPS

COLESLAW

Rae: Noah and I are steadfast about coleslaw: It is a vinegar-based dish and should never be creamy. We know that people who grew up with creamy slaw can be tough to convert, but this snappy version, which gets a nice earthy dimension from the addition of some celery root, has made believers of more than a few formerly mayo-loving customers. The recipe comes from Noah's bubbe Mildred, from his dad's side.

1 head of red cabbage, cored and shredded	¼ cup cider vinegar
1 medium white onion, grated	1 tablespoon fennel seeds
2 large carrots, grated	2 tablespoons (packed) dark brown sugar
1 medium celery root, peeled and grated	4 teaspoons Diamond Crystal kosher salt
½ cup canola oil	Juice of 1 lemon
1 cup distilled white vinegar	4 teaspoons caraway seeds

Combine the cabbage, onion, carrots, and celery root in a large nonreactive bowl. Then combine the oil, vinegars, fennel seeds, brown sugar, and salt in a medium nonreactive saucepan, place it over medium-high heat, and bring to a boil. Reduce the heat and simmer for 15 minutes. Strain the warm dressing over the vegetables and stir to combine. Add the lemon juice and caraway seeds and stir to combine. Cover and refrigerate, stirring the slaw from time to time, for at least 2 days before serving. The coleslaw will keep in the refrigerator for up to 2 weeks.

MAKES 16 CUPS

Mains, Soups & Sides

VEAL SCHNITZEL

Rae: Pounding a lean piece of animal protein, breading it, and frying it is a classic way to make a little meat go a long way. It also happens to be incredibly delicious. We put veal schnitzel on the menu in homage not to Austria, which made the dish famous, but to Israel, where, thanks to immigrants from German-speaking countries, they eat schnitzel like it's going out of style. You can try all sorts of variations on the breading: matzo meal, straight flour, cornmeal, whatever your tastes dictate. Try serving it with a simple frisée-and-watercress salad dressed with olive oil and lemon juice.

2 cups all-purpose flour
1 teaspoon Diamond Crystal kosher salt (plus more to taste)
1 teaspoon freshly ground black pepper (plus more to taste)
3 large eggs
3 cups matzo meal
4 7-ounce veal-breast cutlets, pounded ¼-inch thick
   Mixture of ½ canola oil and ½ extra-virgin olive oil
4 unpeeled garlic cloves, smashed
8 sprigs of thyme
½ cup minced Pickled Green Tomatoes (page 65), for serving
¼ cup minced Preserved Lemons (page 75), for serving

Place the flour, salt, and pepper in a shallow bowl. Beat the eggs in a separate shallow bowl. Place the matzo meal in a third shallow bowl. Dredge the veal cutlets in the flour, shaking off any excess; next dip them in the eggs, and then dredge them in the matzo meal, shaking off any excess.

In a large pan or skillet, heat enough oil to reach halfway up the sides of the veal cutlets over high heat. When the oil is very hot, add 2 of the veal cutlets to the pan. After about 4 minutes, when the veal is browned and slightly crisp around the edges, turn them over.

Add 2 of the garlic cloves and 4 of the thyme sprigs to the pan. Continue frying, moving the pan around gently and using a spoon to carefully baste the top of the veal several times, until the veal is crisp and golden brown all over, 2 to 3 minutes more. Transfer the veal cutlets to paper towels to absorb excess oil and season with salt and pepper to taste. Discard the garlic and thyme, and repeat with the remaining veal, garlic, and thyme.

Garnish each cutlet with the pickled green tomatoes and preserved lemon.

SERVES 4

ROMANIAN STEAK WITH SPRING ONIONS

Noah: I love steak. Really love steak. Just like my dad who, to this day, still coerces me into gnawing every last sinewy morsel from the bone of a rib steak. When we opened Mile End, we discovered that Romanian steak—which is the quintessential Jewish steak—was traditionally made from the humble cut known as the skirt, which is sort of the kosher equivalent to a hanger or flank steak. The glory of the skirt steak is not just that it's full of flavor and relatively cheap, but also that when you sear it on the grill or skillet, it cooks to a gorgeous, crisp-edged medium-rare in just minutes. We serve our Romanian steak with spring onions and a tangy scallion sauce. Try it with a side of our Kasha Varnishkes (pictured here; recipe on page 158).

FOR THE MARINADE:
- 3 tablespoons Spanish paprika
- ¼ cup extra-virgin olive oil
- 3 sprigs of rosemary
- 4 garlic cloves, peeled and cut in half
- 1 2-pound skirt steak, cut into 4 equal-size pieces

FOR COOKING AND SERVING:
- 4 tablespoons canola oil
- Diamond Crystal kosher salt and freshly ground black pepper
- 1 bunch of spring onions or scallions
- 1 recipe Scallion Sauce (page 76)
- Coarse salt, for serving
- Extra-virgin olive oil, for serving

MARINATE THE STEAKS: Mix all the marinade ingredients together in a bowl; toss the steak in the marinade so that they're coated all over. Transfer the steaks and their marinade to a baking dish, cover it, and refrigerate for at least 3 hours or overnight.

COOK THE STEAKS: Working in two batches, heat 2 tablespoons of the oil in a large skillet over high heat. Season 2 of the steaks with salt and pepper; cook the steaks, turning once, until well seared on both sides and cooked to the desired doneness. Transfer the steaks to a cutting board and let them rest for at least 5 minutes. Repeat with 2 more tablespoons of the oil and the remaining 2 steaks.

Pour off all but 1 tablespoon of fat and return the pan to high heat. Add the spring onions and cook, turning once, until lightly charred, 3 to 4 minutes.

To serve, slice the steak against the grain on a deep bias. Then dollop about 1½ tablespoons of the scallion sauce onto a serving plate, spreading it out to cover the center of the plate. Place a couple of the charred spring onions over the sauce, then place the sliced steak on top of the spring onions. Sprinkle with a little coarse salt and drizzle a little olive oil on top.

SERVES 4

BRAISED BRISKET WITH RED WINE & PRUNES

Rae: A tender braised brisket is the traditional Jewish holiday-meal centerpiece. Gil Marks, in the *Encyclopedia of Jewish Food*, speculates that brisket became a Hanukkah staple ages ago in Eastern Europe, when peasants would slaughter their cows just at the onset of winter because they couldn't afford to keep them alive during the cold months. Today brisket is widely recognized as the quintessential Jewish roasting or braising cut, served on Shabbos and holidays everywhere and anytime. A generally tough cut of meat from the breast region of the cow, brisket needs cooking methods with sufficient time and temperature to break down the many strands of connective tissue that course through the rich flesh, which convert it into a gorgeous, meaty, tender food of beauty. Red wine, spiked with a little red wine vinegar and enriched with basic aromatics (celery, onion, and so on), is the main braising liquid in this recipe, which is so simple to execute and tastes even better when prepared a day in advance. Just cool the brisket and store it overnight in the refrigerator, slicing it cold before reheating.

1 first-cut beef brisket (4 to 5 pounds)	3 fresh bay leaves
Diamond Crystal kosher salt and freshly ground black pepper	25 pitted prunes
2 tablespoons canola oil	2 to 3 large onions, peeled and sliced
3 large carrots, peeled and cut into ½-inch pieces	Cloves from 2 heads of garlic, peeled
2 stalks of celery, cut into ¼-inch pieces	2 cups dry red wine
1 tablespoon fresh thyme	¼ cup plus 2 teaspoons red wine vinegar
Leaves of 1 sprig of rosemary, finely chopped	1 14.5-ounce can crushed tomatoes
	⅓ cup (packed) dark brown sugar
	2 cups water or Beef Stock (page 92)
	Pickled Horseradish (page 86), for serving

Preheat the oven to 325°F. Season the brisket on both sides with salt and pepper. Heat the oil in a large skillet over medium-high heat. Sear the brisket until it's well browned on both sides, 5 to 7 minutes per side. Transfer the brisket to a roasting pan, fat side up, along with the carrots, celery, herbs, and prunes.

Add the onions to the skillet and sauté them over medium-high heat until browned. Add the garlic, wine, and ¼ cup of the vinegar and allow the mixture to reduce until the skillet is almost dry. Then stir in the tomatoes, brown sugar, and water or beef stock.

Pour the onion-wine mixture over the brisket. Seal the roasting pan with a double layer of aluminum foil and cook in the oven until fork-tender, 3½ to 4 hours.

Allow the brisket to cool, uncovered, for about 15 minutes. Carefully transfer the brisket to a serving vessel. Remove and discard the bay leaves and use a slotted spoon to remove the prunes; set the prunes aside. Then strain the cooking liquid into a bowl, setting aside 1 cup of the cooked vegetables and discarding the rest. When the fat has risen to the top of the strained cooking liquid, skim it off and then add the reserved cup of cooked vegetables to the bowl, along with ¼ of the reserved prunes.

Transfer the mixture to a blender (or use an immersion blender) and puree it until smooth. Add the remaining 2 teaspoons of red wine vinegar to the pureed sauce and season it with salt and pepper to taste. Coarsely chop the remaining prunes and add them to the sauce.

Slice the brisket thinly, across the grain. Serve with the sauce and horseradish.

SERVES 8 TO 10

SPRING CHICKEN

Noah: The beauty of this dish is that you get not only the super-moistness of brined and smoked chicken breasts but also the snappy crunch of a high roast or sear. Since Rae and I love escarole, and since we're obsessed with figuring out ways to use up old bread, we serve the breasts with a sort of savory escarole fricassee that's thickened with pieces of stale rye. To give that sauce another layer of richness, we add pieces of chicken confit made from the same bird's thighs and legs. But you can skip the confit if you want; this dish will still have plenty of flavor without it.

½ cup fresh English peas
5 tablespoons canola oil
4 portions Smoked Chicken Breast (page 51)
3 scallions, chopped into 1-inch lengths
2 teaspoons chopped fresh thyme
4 cups coarsely chopped escarole, washed and
    drained
2 cups chicken stock
4 heaping tablespoons Chicken Confit
    (optional; page 77)
4 teaspoons spicy brown mustard, such as Gulden's
8 tablespoons Schmaltz Vinaigrette
    (see Golden Beet Salad recipe, page 170)
4 tablespoons chopped fresh chives
3 to 4 slices stale Rye Bread (page 174),
    torn into 1- to 2-inch pieces
    Pinch of Diamond Crystal kosher salt
½ teaspoon fresh lemon juice
½ teaspoon extra-virgin olive oil

Preheat the oven to 200°F.

Bring a small pot of water to a boil. Add the peas. Return to a boil and simmer for 3 to 5 minutes. Remove 1 or 2 from the pot and taste them. When the peas have lost most of their starchiness and taste perceptibly sweeter, they are done. Strain them, and shock them in a bowl of ice water for 5 minutes. Drain and set aside.

Heat 2 tablespoons of the canola oil in a large skillet over medium-high heat and sear the chicken breasts, skin side down, until nicely browned, 3 to 4 minutes. Lower the heat to medium, flip the breasts, and continue searing them until they're heated through, 3 to 4 minutes more. Transfer the breasts to the oven to keep them warm.

Meanwhile, make the sauce: Heat the remaining 3 tablespoons of oil in a very large skillet or saucepan over medium-high heat. Add the scallions and allow them to color slightly. Add the thyme and let it sizzle for a few seconds to flavor the oil. Then add the escarole; toss to coat the leaves with the oil and wilt them slightly, 10 to 15 seconds. Add 1½ cups of the chicken stock and let it come to a brisk simmer.

Add the chicken confit, mustard, and schmaltz vinaigrette; toss to combine thoroughly. Let the sauce simmer and reduce, stirring occasionally, until it's thickened, 4 to 5 minutes. Then add the chives and rye bread. Add the remaining ½ cup of chicken stock and continue to toss and cook for another 20 to 30 seconds, then remove the skillet from the heat.

Remove the chicken breasts from the oven and slice each of them crosswise on a deep bias into 3 roughly equal-size segments. Divide the sauce evenly among 4 serving plates, pooling it in the center of the plate, and place 1 sliced chicken breast on each plate.

In a small bowl, toss the blanched peas with the salt, lemon juice, and olive oil. Sprinkle the peas over the chicken breasts and serve.

SERVES 4

HOT TONGUE ON TOAST

Rae: It took us a while to put a tongue sandwich—that deli classic—on our menu, and I guess you could say we only got partway there. But rest assured, this is the best deconstructed tongue sandwich you'll ever taste. The rich texture of the pickled lamb's tongue, the horseradish notes, the sweetness of the raisin-onion marmalade slathered on toasty pumpernickel are pure pleasure. You can serve this as a very hearty appetizer or a small main course.

FOR THE RAISIN-ONION MARMALADE:

- 3 tablespoons canola oil
- 4 medium red onions, halved and thinly sliced
- 1 tablespoon Diamond Crystal kosher salt
- ½ cup dry red wine
- ¼ cup golden raisins
- ½ teaspoon ground cinnamon
- ½ teaspoon ground ginger
- ¼ teaspoon ground cloves
- ¼ cup (packed) dark brown sugar
- 1 fresh bay leaf
- ¼ cup dry vermouth
- Juice of ½ lemon, for finishing
- ¼ cup chopped flat-leaf parsley, for finishing

FOR THE SANDWICH:

- 6 pieces Pickled Lamb's Tongue (page 46)
- 6 tablespoons canola oil
- 6 slices Pumpernickel Bread (page 174)
- Extra-virgin olive oil
- Diamond Crystal kosher salt
- Freshly grated horseradish root

MAKE THE RAISIN-ONION MARMALADE: Heat the oil in a heavy-bottomed pot or Dutch oven over medium-high heat. Add the onions and salt, and cook over medium heat, stirring frequently, until the onions are softened and translucent, about 10 minutes.

Increase the heat to high, add the wine, and reduce until almost dry. Adjust the heat to medium-low and add all the remaining ingredients except the lemon juice and parsley. Stir to combine. Let the mixture cook, stirring frequently, until almost all the liquid has evaporated and the marmalade has a thick and sticky consistency, about 20 minutes. The marmalade will keep, covered, in the refrigerator, for up to 2 weeks.

PREPARE THE SANDWICHES: Preheat the oven to 200°F.

Slice each tongue in half lengthwise. In a large pan or skillet, heat half the oil over medium heat and then sear half the tongues cut-side down, without moving them, until a light crust develops and the tongues are heated through, about 2 minutes. Flip the tongues, cook them for 30 seconds more, and transfer them to a plate or baking sheet. Keep the tongues warm in the oven. Repeat with the remaining oil and tongues.

Heat the raisin-onion marmalade in a saucepan over medium-low heat; when it's warmed through, add the lemon juice and parsley and stir to combine.

Meanwhile, toast the pumpernickel slices on both sides in a large pan or skillet (in batches, if necessary) in a little olive oil, and sprinkle them with a little salt.

PREPARE THE PLATES: Cut each pumpernickel slice in half, spread a few tablespoons of the warm marmalade on each half, and lay 2 toast halves on each of 6 serving plates. Working with one plate at a time, lay 1 tongue half across one of the pieces of toast, then lay the second piece of toast partially over the first piece of tongue. Finally, lay a second half of tongue over the second toast half. Top it all with a few more tablespoons of the marmalade and some horseradish.

SERVES 6

Nick DiMinno Jr.
Owner, Sip Fine Wine, Brooklyn

Matches Made in Heaven

WHEN YOU THINK ABOUT IT, Jewish cooking, with all its sweet-tart-rich-savory flavors, is a wine lover's dream. So much potential for eye-opening pairings! So much pleasure! What a shame that for so long wine was brought to the Jewish table only as a sacrament at best, and an afterthought at worst. This is a cuisine that cries out for good wine, and frankly, finding the right bottles to go with Mile End's food—something Noah, Rae, and I work on together (if you can call it work) whenever we get the chance—reminds me why I got into the wine business in the first place. Always, I go in with an open mind, free of preconceived ideas about how the wine should be made. (Kosher? Fine, if it's tasty. Organic? Sure, but because it's good, not just because it's virtuous.) Beyond that, I just stick to some basic principles of choosing and pairing:

1. BALANCE IS EVERYTHING. No matter what dish you're serving, no matter whether you're drinking red, white, or rosé, seek out a wine in which no single trait—be it sweetness or acidity or fruitiness or oakiness—drowns out the others.

2. PAIR LIGHT WITH LIGHT, HEAVY WITH HEAVY. Look for a wine that will neither overpower the food you're serving nor be overpowered by it. The delicate flavor of fresh fish will be all but obliterated by a rich, full-bodied Cabernet, just as a hearty beef stew will stomp all over the crisp, citrusy aromas of a nice Sauvignon Blanc. Swap those two pairings and all will be love and harmony!

3. PAIR FRUIT WITH SPICE. Food with a little heat calls not for a peppery or spicy wine but for a fruit-forward one.

4. PAIR ACID WITH FAT. Wines with a tart or bracing acidity offer a pleasing counterpoint to rich and fatty foods like soft cheeses.

As far as I'm concerned, if you've got those fundamentals under your belt, you're ready for some seriously good eating and drinking. Speaking of which, here are some pairing suggestions for a few of Mile End's signature dishes:

VEAL SCHNITZEL (PAGE 136)

When I think schnitzel, I think Austria, and when I think about Mile End's elegant take on the breaded veal cutlet—with its intensely tart preserved lemons and tangy pickled green tomatoes—I think of Austrian wine, especially its dominant varietals, Grüner Veltliner and Riesling. Here I'd go with a Grüner or Riesling that is neither too dry nor too sweet—that is, one with enough residual sugar to complement the sour elements in the dish, but also enough acidic backbone to stand up to the sweet, buttery flavors of the veal.

ROMANIAN STEAK WITH SPRING ONIONS (PAGE 139)

As a rule, steak is relatively easy to pair with wine—go big, go red—but the sweet smoked paprika in the marinade for Mile End's skirt steak requires a little customization. For me, that sweet paprika immediately calls to mind its country of origin, Spain, which in turn calls to mind the bold, tempranillo-based wines of Ribera del Duero. A good Ribera has just the right amount of fruit concentration and structure to complement seared marinated meats. By the same token, the steak's nicely seared crust calls to mind smoke and char, which calls to mind—my mind, at least—volcanoes, which in turn calls to mind the inky wines born in the volcanic soils of Sicily and Basilicata—specifically the former's Nero d'Avolas and the latter's Aglianicos. Both are fine companions for this steak.

BRAISED BRISKET WITH RED WINE & PRUNES (PAGE 140)

When you have a glorious joint of dense, fatty protein that's been slow-cooked with fruit, herbs, and dry red wine, you need a big, tannic, earthy wine with its own stewed-fruit and herb notes. Those traits are the calling card of the famed Syrah-Grenache blends from the southern Rhône villages of Vacqueyras, Gigondas, and Châteauneuf-du-Pape. Those exalted French wines can get expensive, though, and are somewhat tough when young, but don't worry: A moderately priced Australian Shiraz can deliver equally great pleasure with this dish.

PAN-SEARED TROUT

Noah: Trout is a wonder fish. It's got delicate, slightly sweet flesh that sears beautifully, and a single fish is usually just the right size to make a perfect dinner for one (or a light dinner for two). Plus, trout swims in lakes and rivers, meaning you can buy it fresh even in landlocked parts of the country. We get ours from Eden Brook Trout, an excellent fishery about a hundred miles from New York City.

Still, it's not the most Jewish of fish choices, so we serve ours with horseradish cream, partly as a way to back the trout into a more Jewish tradition, and also to give it some richness. Then we garnish the fish with salty-sweet quick-cured shallots and tangy pickled beets; trout takes nicely to both, because it's a fairly neutral-tasting fish. For our entrée, we butterfly a whole trout after removing the head, tail, dorsal fin, and bones, which makes for a really pretty presentation. Just ask your fishmonger to do it for you.

4 tablespoons canola oil
4 1-pound rainbow trout, cleaned, deboned, and butterflied
Diamond Crystal kosher salt
Horseradish Cream (page 90), for serving
Pickled Beets (page 72), for serving
Extra-virgin olive oil
Salt Shallots (page 76), for serving
Fresh tarragon leaves, for serving

Heat 1 tablespoon of the canola oil in a nonstick skillet over high heat. Working with one butterflied trout at a time, sprinkle both sides of the fish generously with salt and place it in the skillet, skin side down. Cook the fish until the skin is crisp and seared around the edges and the flesh is almost entirely opaque except for a bit of pink along the centerline of each fillet, 6 to 8 minutes. Turn the fish flesh side down and sear it for 5 to 10 seconds. Transfer the fish to a warm plate and repeat with the remaining oil and trout.

To serve, dollop a generous spoonful of horseradish cream onto the center of a plate and spread it around a bit; place the trout skin side up on top of the horseradish cream. Place a tablespoon or two of pickled beets in a small bowl, drizzle them with a little olive oil, and stir to coat; distribute the beets evenly over the trout. Scatter a tablespoon or so of the salt shallots and some tarragon leaves over the trout and drizzle it with a little more olive oil. Repeat with the remaining trout and garnishes.

SERVES 4

CHICKEN SOUP & ITS VARIATIONS

Noah: It's my earliest cooking memory: standing on a stool next to my grandmother as she presided over a pot of chicken soup on the stove. Nana would talk me through it: a little salt, a little pepper, turn down the heat, stir, simmer. I went through a long phase as a kid of eating only chicken soup and Cheerios. Chicken soup was as vital to me as water and air. Sure, there was brisket on some Fridays, or knishes and cauliflower pie on others, but there was always chicken soup. My Nana would have a supply in her freezer, enough to feed the Canadian army. There was always a piece of carrot in her soup, and a large stalk of celery, and some onions. It was simple and pure. It was my first love.

Frankly, we were afraid to do chicken soup at Mile End at first, because we didn't want to compete with all those memories—not just my own, but also the memories of all those customers who grew up loving their bubbes' soups. Plus, Rae had her own sacred family recipe— her great-grandparents were chicken farmers in New Jersey, for God's sake. Hers was greener, with tons of dill.

Eventually, though, we decided to go for it and came up with a wonderfully rich soup, made not just with bones but with whole chickens. You can pull that meat off once it's cooked and use it for Chicken Salad (page 125) or add it back into the soup at the end, if you want. As for what else to put in it—aside from the requisite carrots, onions, and celery—we usually go for the gusto and add a trifecta of matzo balls, kreplach, and crunchy house-baked soup mandel. Why skimp? Really, you can add almost anything you like.

recipe continues ➜

3 small chickens (about 2½ pounds each), each cut into 8 pieces
10 black peppercorns
2 teaspoons Diamond Crystal kosher salt, plus more to taste
4 medium parsnips, peeled, 2 left whole and 2 cut into 2- to 3-inch batons
4 medium carrots, peeled, 2 left whole and 2 cut into 2- to 3-inch batons
4 stalks of celery, trimmed, 2 left whole and 2 cut into 2- to 3-inch batons
3 large onions, peeled, 2 cut in half and 1 coarsely chopped
3 sprigs of dill
3 sprigs of flat-leaf parsley
3 sprigs of thyme
2 fresh bay leaves
   Matzo Balls (optional; page 155)
   Kreplach (optional; page 154)
   Cooked Egg Noodles (optional; page 84)
   Soup Mandel (page 90), for garnish

Place the chicken pieces in a large stockpot along with the peppercorns, salt, and enough water to cover the ingredients by about 2 inches. Heat the pot over medium heat until the contents of the pot start to simmer. Adjust the heat to maintain a low simmer and continue cooking, uncovered, for about 1½ hours, occasionally skimming off any foam and fat that rise to the top.

Using a slotted spoon or tongs, remove the breast and thigh sections and reserve them for the soup (or another use, like chicken salad), leaving the drumsticks and wings in the pot. Add the 2 whole parsnips, 2 whole carrots, 2 whole celery stalks, and 2 halved onions to the pot and continue to simmer for another 1½ hours, stirring and skimming occasionally.

Remove the pot from the heat and add the dill, parsley, thyme, and bay leaves. Allow the herbs to steep for 30 minutes. Then strain the stock through a fine mesh sieve, discarding the solids.

Return the strained soup to the pot and bring it to a low simmer. Add the parsnip, carrot, and celery batons; chopped onions; and matzo balls. Simmer for another 15 minutes, then add the kreplach, along with some of the reserved breast and thigh meat, if you like. Simmer for 5 minutes more and season to taste. Place the egg noodles in bowls, ladle the soup over them, and serve with soup mandel.

SERVES 6 TO 8 AS AN ENTRÉE

KREPLACH

Rae: I'm sure at one point in history matzo balls and kreplach shared power equally in the royal court of Jewish cooking, but somehow, over time, the matzo ball became queen—it even gave its name to the most popular of Jewish chicken soups. But I think these lovely meat dumplings are due for a comeback. Even when made with store-bought wonton wrappers, which is how we make them, tender kreplach floating in home-made chicken soup are transcendent.

½ tablespoon canola oil
 2 tablespoons chopped shallots
½ pound raw boneless chicken meat
¼ pound chicken skin and fat
 2 chicken livers
 2 garlic cloves, minced
¼ cup chopped fresh chives
1¼ teaspoons Diamond Crystal kosher salt
¾ teaspoon freshly ground black pepper
20 to 25 square wonton wrappers

Heat the oil in a small pan or skillet over medium heat, add the shallots, and cook them until softened, 2 to 3 minutes. Add the shallots to the bowl of a food processor along with the chicken meat, chicken skin and fat, livers, and garlic. Process for 30 to 45 seconds. Scrape down the sides of the bowl and add the chives, salt, and pepper. Pulse a few times to combine.

Dollop about 2 teaspoons of the filling in the center of a wonton wrapper. Brush the edges with water, then fold the corners of the wrapper together and crimp the edges, forcing out as much air as possible. Press the tines of a fork into the crimped edges to make a decorative pattern if you like. Repeat with the remaining filling and wrappers.

To cook, simply add the kreplach to a large pot of soup at a low, steady simmer 4 to 5 minutes before the soup is ready to serve. (The kreplach can be frozen on a baking sheet and transferred to a container; they will keep frozen for about 2 months. You can add them to the soup frozen; in that case, cook for an additional 5 minutes.)

MAKES ABOUT 20 (ENOUGH FOR ROUGHLY
6 ENTRÉE SERVINGS OF CHICKEN SOUP, PAGE 151)

MATZO BALLS

Noah: These fluffy matzo balls can be cooked right in our chicken soup, or, for especially flavorful ones, cook them separately in chicken stock and add them to the soup right before serving. And keep in mind: When you're rolling them, you're not making a meatball. You don't want them to be too tight and dense, so use a gentle touch.

1⅓ cups matzo meal
4 large eggs
⅓ cup Schmaltz (page 91)
¼ teaspoon Diamond Crystal kosher salt
¼ teaspoon freshly ground black pepper
1 tablespoon baking powder
8 cups chicken stock (if not cooking the matzo balls in the Chicken Soup, page 151)

Thoroughly mix all the ingredients except the chicken stock together in a large bowl. Cover and refrigerate for 2 hours. (You can make the mixture a day ahead; you'll need to store it in a sealed container that has enough room to allow the mixture to expand.)

Form the matzo mixture into balls that are a little larger than a quarter; they should be completely smooth on the outside with no cracks. Cook the matzo balls in barely simmering chicken stock for 20 minutes, or just add the balls to your chicken soup 20 minutes or so before serving (around the same time you'd put the vegetables in; see page 151), keeping the soup at a low, steady simmer.

MAKES ABOUT 10

BORSCHT

Rae: What I love about our updated version of this peasant soup is that it's based on an actual beet broth—not beef stock, as in a lot of Russian borschts, and not even vegetable stock to which beets have been added. This is a really beet-y, and surprisingly hearty, borscht. And it's completely vegetarian.

FOR THE BEET STOCK:

- 6 cups water
- 1 large onion, chopped
- 1 pound beets (about 2 medium beets), peeled and grated
- 1 medium carrot, peeled and grated
- 4 stalks of celery, trimmed and chopped
- 2 Beefsteak or Jersey tomatoes, chopped
- 3 whole allspice berries
- 2 teaspoons dill seeds
- 1 fresh bay leaf
- 2 or 3 sprigs of parsley
- 2 or 3 sprigs of dill
- 1 sprig of thyme

FOR THE SOUP:

- 1 tablespoon canola oil
- 1 bunch Tuscan kale or chard, thick stems removed, cut into ribbons
- 1 carrot, grated
- ¼ head of green cabbage, trimmed and thinly sliced
- Diamond Crystal kosher salt and freshly ground black pepper
- Lemon juice, for serving
- Crème fraîche, for serving

MAKE THE BEET STOCK: Combine all the stock ingredients in a large pot and bring to a boil; reduce the heat and simmer, covered, for 1½ to 2 hours. When the stock is cool enough to handle, strain it through a fine mesh sieve, pressing down on the mixture to extract all the liquid. Discard the solids and set the stock aside; it can be stored in the refrigerator for up to a week.

MAKE THE SOUP: Pour the oil into a large pot; place it over medium heat and add the kale, carrot, and cabbage. Cook, stirring frequently, until the kale and cabbage are al dente. Pour the reserved stock into the pot and stir. Season with salt and pepper to taste. Serve the borscht hot; finish each bowl with a squeeze of lemon juice and a little crème fraîche.

SERVES 6

KASHA VARNISHKES

Noah: When I was a kid, it was the noodles I wanted, not the healthy buckwheat grains, and to this day I still think of this as a pasta dish. Rae prefers the grains, and she arguably loves kasha varnishkes more than I do—her dog's name was Kasha Varnishkes Cohen. For the Mile End version (pictured with the Romanian Steak on page 138), we enrich the dish with gizzard confit or chicken confit and give it an earthy dimension with chanterelle mushrooms.

1 **cup medium-grain kasha**

1 **large egg**

3 **tablespoons rendered duck fat or Schmaltz (page 91)**

2 **cups chicken stock**

   Diamond Crystal kosher salt

1 **large onion, sliced**

1 **pound chanterelle or other mushrooms, cleaned and cut in half**

1 **recipe Gizzard Confit (page 77) or ½ cup Chicken Confit (page 77)**

5 **cups cooked homemade Egg Noodles (page 84)**
   or cooked store-bought egg noodles, for serving
   Freshly ground black pepper

3 **tablespoons tarragon leaves, for serving**

Combine the kasha, egg, and 1 tablespoon of the duck fat in a bowl and mix well.

Pour the stock into a small saucepan and bring it to a boil; season lightly with salt and keep the broth hot.

Transfer the kasha mixture to a pan or skillet and cook it over medium heat, stirring frequently, until the grains are firm and smell like toasted nuts, 1 to 2 minutes. Reduce the heat to low and slowly pour the hot broth into the skillet. Simmer, covered, until the kasha is fully cooked, 5 to 7 minutes.

In a sauté pan, heat 1 tablespoon of the duck fat over medium-high heat. Add the onion and cook, stirring occasionally, until it starts to brown, 5 to 7 minutes. Add the remaining tablespoon of duck fat along with the mushrooms and cook, stirring frequently, for 5 more minutes. Remove the gizzards or chicken legs from their fat and add them to the pan; cook until they're warmed through. Season with salt and pepper. Then add the cooked kasha and noodles and stir to combine. Garnish with the tarragon.

SERVES 6

TSIMIS

Rae: This is an old-timey High Holiday vegetable side dish (pictured on the following page), sweetened with honey and raisins or prunes and, sadly, often simmered to mushy blandness. To get past that problem, roast the carrots first, to brown them and coax out their natural sweetness, and then bring everything together on the stove top at the end. Sunflower seeds add a nutty note to the chewy prunes and raisins.

2 pounds carrots (about 6 large carrots), peeled and cut into ¼-inch coins
2 tablespoons canola oil
1 teaspoon Diamond Crystal kosher salt, plus more to taste
¼ teaspoon freshly ground black pepper, plus more to taste
1 cup honey
    Juice of 2 lemons
3 sprigs of thyme
1 cup quartered pitted prunes
½ cup golden raisins
½ teaspoon ground ginger
¼ teaspoon ground cinnamon
¾ cup sunflower seeds, toasted
    Chopped fresh flat-leaf parsley, for garnish

Preheat the oven to 350°F.

In a roasting pan, toss the carrots with the oil, salt, and pepper. Cook in the oven, stirring occasionally, until the carrots are lightly browned and somewhat tender, 40 to 50 minutes.

Meanwhile, combine the honey, juice from 1½ lemons (reserve the remaining lemon half), thyme, and ⅓ cup water in a large pan or skillet. Bring to a simmer and cook the mixture over medium-high heat for 5 minutes, then remove and discard the thyme. Remove the pan from the heat.

When the carrots are done cooking, pour the carrots, prunes, and raisins into the pan with the honey mixture and stir to coat completely.

Add the ginger and cinnamon, and simmer the carrot-honey mixture over medium-high heat, stirring frequently, until the liquid has reduced to a thick glaze, 10 to 15 minutes. Then add the sunflower seeds and juice from the remaining ½ lemon and remove the pan from the heat. Season with salt and pepper to taste. Garnish with the chopped parsley.

SERVES 6

Left: Tsimis, *Right:* Brussels Sprouts

BRUSSELS SPROUTS

Rae: This fall dish is about as tailored to the season as you can get. It brings together Brussels sprouts, so cheap and plentiful in the fall, with honey, nuts, and apples, which are symbolic foods of the High Holidays. The sweetness from the honey could turn even the pickiest eater into a Brussels believer, and the best part is that you can prepare the Brussels sprouts and walnuts ahead of time and finish them off in a skillet with the apples right before serving.

FOR THE CANDIED WALNUTS:

- 1 tablespoon unsalted butter or canola oil
- ¼ cup walnut pieces
- 1 teaspoon Diamond Crystal kosher salt
  Leaves from 2 sprigs of rosemary
- 2 tablespoons honey

FOR THE BRUSSELS SPROUTS AND APPLES:

- 1½ pounds Brussels sprouts (about 2 pints), cut in half
- 1 tablespoon canola oil
- 1 teaspoon Diamond Crystal kosher salt
  Pinch of freshly ground black pepper
- 1 tablespoon unsalted butter or extra-virgin olive oil
- 2 Granny Smith apples, peeled and cut into ½-inch pieces
  Juice of 1 lemon

MAKE THE CANDIED WALNUTS: Heat the butter or oil in a small skillet over medium heat and add the walnut pieces and salt. Cook, stirring frequently, until the walnuts start to take on a light golden color; add the rosemary and cook for 1 minute more. Add the honey, stir, and remove from the heat.

Meanwhile, preheat the oven to 450°F.

MAKE THE BRUSSELS SPROUTS AND APPLES: Toss the Brussels sprouts with the canola oil, salt, and pepper. Spread them out on a 10-by-15-inch baking sheet and roast them until crisp-tender, 12 to 15 minutes. Set aside.

To finish the dish, heat the butter or olive oil in a large skillet over medium-high heat, add the apple pieces, and cook them until lightly browned, about 2 minutes. Add the candied walnuts, Brussels sprouts, and lemon juice, and toss to combine. Adjust the seasoning if needed.

SERVES 4

An afternoon at Mile End

KNISHES

Noah: My Nana Lee made legendary knishes, and she was the inspiration for the kind we make at Mile End. Ours look a little different from traditional round knishes, but once you get the hang of rolling and trimming the dough, they're easy to make. They're adaptable, too: The standard potato filling can be enhanced with almost anything— truffled mushrooms, corned beef and cabbage, whatever leftovers you have in the fridge. And you can top your knishes with all sorts of savory garnishes: caraway seeds, fresh herbs, chopped nuts, and more.

FOR THE FILLING:

- 2 pounds russet potatoes (about 4 potatoes), scrubbed clean
- 1½ pounds Yukon gold potatoes (6 to 8 potatoes), scrubbed clean
- 2 parsnips, peeled and roughly chopped
- ½ celery root, peeled, trimmed, and roughly chopped
- 2 medium white onions, roughly chopped
- 3 tablespoons Schmaltz (page 91) or canola oil
- 2 fresh bay leaves
  Diamond Crystal kosher salt and freshly ground black pepper
- 3 large eggs

FOR THE KNISH DOUGH:

- 8 large eggs, beaten
- ¾ cup Schmaltz (page 91), at room temperature, or canola oil (see Note)
- 5⅓ cups all-purpose flour
- 4 teaspoons baking powder
- 2 teaspoons Diamond Crystal kosher salt
- 1 additional large egg, beaten, for the egg wash
  Poppy seeds, sesame seeds, caraway seeds, or other toppings of your choice
  Spicy brown mustard, such as Gulden's, for serving

MAKE THE FILLING: Preheat the oven to 375°F.

Bake the russet and Yukon gold potatoes on a 10-by-15-inch baking sheet until a small knife meets no resistance when piercing the center of the potatoes, 60 to 90 minutes. Set the potatoes aside to cool.

Meanwhile, place the parsnips, celery root, and onions in a food processor and pulse them until finely chopped. Heat the schmaltz or oil in a large sauté pan over medium heat, add the chopped vegetables and the bay leaves, and season with salt and pepper to taste. Cover and cook for about 15 minutes, stirring frequently, until the vegetables are completely tender, then uncover and cook for another 10 minutes to let the liquid evaporate. Remove from the heat; discard the bay leaves.

recipe continues ➔

When the potatoes are cool enough to handle, peel them and pass them through a ricer into the sautéed vegetable mixture. Add the eggs and season with more salt and pepper; stir with a wooden spoon until the ingredients are thoroughly mixed together. Let cool before forming the knishes.

MAKE THE DOUGH: Place 8 beaten eggs and the schmaltz or oil in the bowl of a stand mixer fitted with the paddle attachment. Combine the flour, baking powder, and salt in a large bowl and add the mixture to the bowl of the stand mixer. Mix on low speed until the dry ingredients are mostly incorporated. Increase the speed to medium and mix until the dough has a smooth, consistent texture, about 1 minute more.

Wrap the dough loosely in plastic wrap and flatten it into a disk. Refrigerate for at least 1 hour or as long as overnight. (The dough can also be frozen for up to 3 weeks; thaw it in the refrigerator overnight before proceeding.)

ROLL AND TRIM THE DOUGH: 1. Portion the dough approximately into thirds. **2.** Flatten one-third with a rolling pin or the palm of your hand to approximately ¼ inch thick. **3.** Pass it through a pasta machine at the widest setting. Fold the dough in half, if necessary, and pass it through the rollers 1 or 2 more times until the results yield a piece that is close to the width of the machine (about 6 inches). **4.** Adding flour as necessary to prevent sticking, continue to pass the dough through the machine, making the setting more narrow with each pass until you achieve a piece that is approximately ¹⁄₁₆ inch thick. **5.** Place the dough on a floured surface and cut it into squares. Reserve the trimmings and incorporate into the next piece of dough to be rolled. Repeat with the other two-thirds of the dough.

STUFF AND BAKE THE KNISHES: Preheat the oven to 375°F. Lightly oil a 10-by-15-inch baking sheet. **6.** Distribute about 1 cup of the filling evenly along one edge of a trimmed dough piece. **7.** Roll the dough around the filling to make a cylinder, using a spatula to help lift the bottom of the dough from the work surface where the dough is sticking. **8.** Brush the seam of the rolled knish with the egg wash and press lightly to seal it. Place the knish seam-side down on the prepared baking sheet. Repeat with the remaining dough pieces and filling. **9.** Make 4 or 5 diagonal slashes across the top of each knish to allow for expansion while cooking. Brush each knish with a little of the egg wash and sprinkle it with the topping of your choice. Bake until golden brown, 20 to 25 minutes. Allow to cool slightly before serving. Slice each knish into 4 small logs and serve with the mustard.

NOTE: *If you use oil instead of schmaltz, reduce the flour to 5 cups.*

TIP: *If you don't have any schmaltz on hand, you can buy duck fat at most specialty-food stores.*

MAKES 12

KNISHES, STEP BY STEP

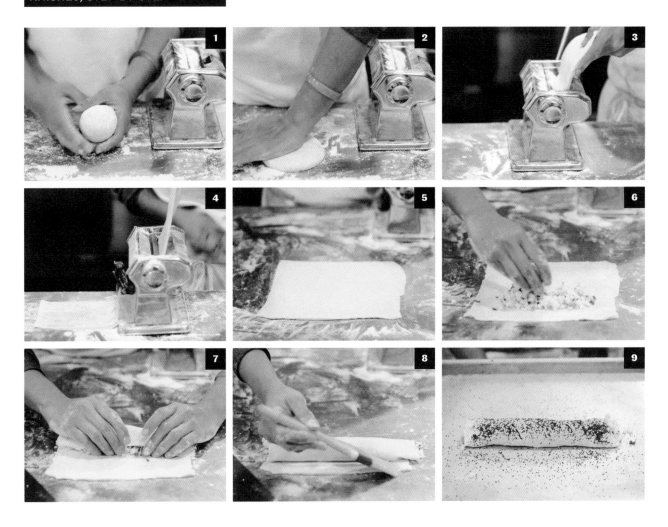

LATKES

Noah: We make a pretty classic potato pancake to use as the crisp base for our Mont Royal breakfast special (page 101), but I actually prefer non-potato versions, with butternut squash, say, or celery root and parsnips. You can use the same basic recipe for all of them, with just a few minor adjustments. Then there are the accompaniments: caviar and sour cream with the sweeter butternut squash latkes, Horseradish Cream (page 90) with the celery-root version and, of course, the traditional pairing of Applesauce (page 80) with the classic potato-chive ones. We've served a quince compote with our latkes, too—almost any fall fruit, stewed down, will taste great with any kind of latke. Note that this recipe suggests making pretty small latkes, which are easier to fry up, but if you're making them for the Mont Royal, you'll want to form bigger ones, about the size of the palm of your hand. Finally, I recommend using a food processor with a grating disk over grating by hand if you're making a sizable batch. I'm old-school, but not that old-school.

VERSION 1: **Potato Latkes**

- 2 pounds russet potatoes, peeled and coarsely grated
- 1 medium onion, grated
- 1¼ cups matzo meal
- ¾ cup chopped fresh chives
- 5 large eggs
- 1 tablespoon Diamond Crystal kosher salt
- ¾ teaspoon freshly ground black pepper
- Canola oil

Place the grated potatoes in a large bowl or other food-safe container, fill it with water, and then strain. Repeat this rinsing process 2 or 3 times until the water runs clear, then drain the potatoes, squeezing out as much water as possible.

Combine the rinsed potatoes and grated onion in a large bowl and mix them together with your hands. Add the matzo meal and mix together, then add the chives. Finally, add the eggs and massage them into the potato mixture until thoroughly incorporated. Add the salt and pepper and mix it in with your hands.

Heat 2 to 3 tablespoons of oil in a large skillet over medium heat. Working in batches so that the latkes are not crowded in the skillet, take a golf ball–size portion of the potato mixture, flatten it between the palms of your hands, and add it to the skillet. Repeat. Cook the latkes until they're crisp and brown around the edges, about 3 minutes; then flip and cook for another 2 to 3 minutes, until crisp and deep golden brown all over and still tender inside. Transfer to a paper towel–lined plate or baking sheet. Repeat with the remaining potato mixture, adding a tablespoon or so of oil between batches.

VERSION 2: **Celery Root–Parsnip Latkes**

- 1 pound celery root, peeled and grated
- 1 pound parsnips, grated
- 1 medium onion, grated
- 1¼ cups matzo meal
- ¾ cup chopped fresh flat-leaf parsley
- 5 large eggs
- 1 tablespoon Diamond Crystal kosher salt
- ¾ teaspoon freshly ground black pepper
  Canola oil

Follow the instructions for the potato version, substituting the celery root and parsnips for the potatoes (and skipping the rinsing step at the beginning) and substituting the parsley for the chives.

VERSION 3: **Butternut Squash Latkes**

- 1 3- to 4-pound butternut squash, peeled, seeds and pith removed
- 1 medium onion, grated
- 1 cup matzo meal
- ⅓ cup chopped fresh sage
- 5 large eggs
- 1 teaspoon Diamond Crystal kosher salt
- ½ teaspoon freshly ground black pepper
  Canola oil

Cut the squash into chunks and pass them through the grating disk of a food processor. Then follow the instructions for the potato version, substituting the squash for the potatoes (and skipping the rinsing step at the beginning) and substituting the sage for the chives, and cooking the latkes slightly longer over slightly lower heat (about 4 minutes on the first side and 3 minutes on the second side over medium-low heat).

You can reheat the latkes in a 450°F oven in 3 to 4 minutes.

MAKES 25 TO 30 SMALL LATKES

GOLDEN BEET SALAD WITH SCHMALTZ VINAIGRETTE

Noah: This is one of my favorite things on Mile End's menu. It marries so many of my favorite traditional elements of Jewish cooking: beets, those classic root vegetables of shtetl life; schmaltz; plus the crunchy gribenes garnish—it's pure deliciousness. In the deli we serve this as a salad course, but it works equally well as a side dish as part of a larger meal. When seasoning the beets, keep in mind that you have to be a little more generous to bring out their sweet, earthy quality. You can use red beets instead of golden ones if you want, but you won't get the same elegant, understated appearance, and they will cause the plate to turn purple.

FOR THE BEET SALAD:
- 10 small-to-medium golden beets, cleaned but not peeled
- 10 to 12 sprigs of thyme
- 1 tablespoon Diamond Crystal kosher salt, plus more to taste
- ¼ cup plus 2 tablespoons canola oil
- ¼ cup water
- 3 leeks, white parts only, washed and trimmed
- Juice of 2 lemons
- ½ cup chopped fresh flat-leaf parsley
- Gribenes (page 91), for garnish
- 1 cup Champagne grapes, for garnish

FOR THE SCHMALTZ VINAIGRETTE:
- ½ cup Schmaltz (page 91)
- 1 small shallot, minced
- 1 tablespoon spicy brown mustard, such as Gulden's
- ½ teaspoon sugar
- 1 tablespoon Champagne vinegar
- 1 teaspoon Diamond Crystal kosher salt

MAKE THE BEET SALAD: Preheat the oven to 400°F.

Combine the beets, thyme, salt, and ¼ cup of the oil in a large bowl and toss until the beets are thoroughly coated with the oil. Transfer the mixture to a roasting pan along with the water. Cover it tightly with foil and cook in the oven until a knife inserted into one of the beets meets no resistance, about 1 hour.

MAKE THE SCHMALTZ VINAIGRETTE: Vigorously whisk all the vinaigrette ingredients together in a bowl. Set aside.

Transfer the roasted beets to a bowl, discard the thyme, cover the bowl with plastic wrap, and let the beets steam for 20 minutes. When they're cool enough to handle (but still very warm), peel the beets. Set the peeled beets aside.

Meanwhile, blanch the leeks in lightly salted boiling water for 5 to 6 minutes, then transfer them to an ice-water bath for a minute or so. Pat the leeks dry and cut them in half lengthwise.

Heat the remaining 2 tablespoons of oil in a large sauté pan or skillet over medium-high heat and sear the leeks, cut side down, without moving them, until they're lightly charred, about 2 minutes. Transfer the leeks to a cutting board and cut them on the bias into 3 equal-size segments.

Slice the roasted, peeled beets in half from root to stem, and then slice each half into 4 wedges. Transfer the sliced beets to a large bowl along with the lemon juice and salt to taste. Add the parsley and ¼ cup of the schmaltz vinaigrette and toss to combine. (You can reserve any leftover vinaigrette for another use.) Divide the dressed beets evenly among 6 serving plates.

In the same bowl, very gently toss the charred, sliced leeks, letting them pick up whatever vinaigrette is left in the bowl. Divide the dressed leeks evenly among the 6 plates, laying them on top of the beets. Sprinkle the salads with gribenes and garnish them with the Champagne grapes.

SERVES 6

Rye Bread

Breads

RYE & PUMPERNICKEL BREAD

Noah: A big part of my dream of opening a deli was baking rye bread—one that would be worthy of our smoked meat—in-house. But, alas, my baking skills are limited, and the patience needed to make quality rye wasn't in my repertoire. Along came Rich Maggi, a cook with many years of experience on the line, whose dream it was to bake. And boy, can this guy bake. A sandwich on mediocre bread will always be a mediocre sandwich regardless of what's inside. Rich knew that, and set out to turn what were already great sandwiches into some of the city's best.

Today we make our rye using plenty of rye flour and real, living sourdough starter made from airborne yeast cultures, which gives the bread an incredible depth of flavor. If you don't have your own sourdough starter, that's fine: This recipe shows you how to make a quick starter, called a poolish, using instant yeast. Most Montreal delis serve their smoked meat on unseeded rye, but I wanted Rich to create a seeded loaf, because I love the aromatic profile those caraway seeds bring to the mix. We use just enough to impart that distinctive taste and aroma.

We also make a rich, slightly sweet pumpernickel for our corned beef, using the same basic recipe (the instructions below explain the extra ingredients and steps for making pumpernickel). These breads will stay good sitting out for up to one week—just spray a bit of water on the bread and bring it back to life in a warm oven. Heavenly.

FOR THE POOLISH:
- ¼ teaspoon instant yeast
- ½ cup dark rye flour
- ½ cup lukewarm water

FOR THE DOUGH:
- 1 cup lukewarm water
- ½ teaspoon instant yeast
- 1 tablespoon (packed) light or dark brown sugar
- 1 tablespoon canola oil
- 1½ tablespoons caraway seeds
- 3¼ cups all-purpose flour
- 1 teaspoon Diamond Crystal kosher salt
  Cornmeal, for coating the baking sheet

ADDITIONAL INGREDIENTS FOR PUMPERNICKEL:
- ½ tablespoons caramel color (see Note)
- ¾ tablespoon yellow mustard seeds
- ¼ cup raisins, soaked in water for 1 hour and strained

MAKE THE POOLISH: Combine the yeast, rye flour, and lukewarm water in a large bowl and whisk until the mixture is smooth and has the consistency of pancake batter. Cover it loosely with plastic wrap and refrigerate for at least 1 day and up to 1 week.

MAKE THE DOUGH: Combine ¼ cup of the poolish (reserving the rest for another use) in the bowl of a stand mixer with the water, yeast, brown sugar, canola oil, and caraway seeds. If you're making pumpernickel, add the caramel color, mustard seeds, and raisins now, too. With a rubber spatula or spoon, mix to combine.

Add the flour and salt. Using the dough-hook attachment, mix on medium speed until the dough starts to pull away cleanly from the sides of the bowl, about 5 to 7 minutes. Stop the mixer and let the dough rest for 5 minutes. Then continue mixing until the dough is smooth, about 5 minutes more.

On a floured work surface, knead the dough gently for 15 to 20 seconds and form it into a ball. Place the dough ball in a bowl greased with cooking spray. Cover the bowl with plastic wrap and let it rest in a warm, draft-free area until roughly doubled in size, 1 to 2 hours.

Transfer the dough to a floured work surface and use your fingertips to gently flatten the ball into a thick disk about 6 inches across. Then, starting with the edge closest to you, roll the disk into a tight cylinder, tucking in the ends of the cylinder as you go. Place the dough, seam side down, onto a 10-by-15-inch baking sheet sprinkled with cornmeal. Spray the top of the dough lightly with cooking spray (to prevent sticking), cover the dough with plastic wrap, and let it rest in a warm, draft-free area until roughly doubled in size, 1 to 2 hours. (To test if it's ready for baking, poke the loaf with a lightly floured finger. If it's ready, a slight depression will remain; if it's not, it will bounce back.)

BAKE THE BREAD: Preheat the oven to 425°F and place a roasting pan containing a cup or so of water in the bottom of the oven (to provide a little steam during the first part of baking).

Uncover the dough and, using a large knife, score the top of the dough deeply on the diagonal 3 times, with the blade entering the dough at a roughly 45-degree angle.

Bake, rotating the tray 180 degrees halfway through cooking, until a thermometer inserted into the center of the loaf reads 190°F, 18 to 20 minutes. Let the bread cool completely before slicing.

NOTE: *You can find caramel color in a supermarket with a West Indian section.*

MAKES ONE 1½-POUND LOAF

CHALLAH

Noah: The best challahs, in my opinion, are the ones that straddle bread and cake; they should have a sweet, super-moist crumb—you should be able to squish a piece into a dense little square, like my sister and I used to do as kids—and a glossy crust. It's a celebratory Shabbos bread, after all. The challah dough also makes our Pletzel (page 184) and our Cinnamon Buns (page 115). This recipe will yield just the right amount of dough for either of those preparations, though you can also easily double the recipe and divide the dough into two batches prior to rising. Leftover challah is also great for French toast and for its delicious cousin, Twice-Baked Challah (page 116).

1¼ cups lukewarm water

1 large egg, at room temperature

1 large egg yolk, at room temperature

2 teaspoons instant yeast

1 tablespoon canola oil

¼ cup sugar

4 cups bread flour

1 teaspoon Diamond Crystal kosher salt

1 additional large egg, beaten, for the egg wash (if making a braided loaf)

¼ cup sesame seeds or poppy seeds (if making a braided loaf)

MAKE THE DOUGH: Combine the water, egg, egg yolk, yeast, oil, and sugar in the bowl of a stand mixer; whisk the ingredients by hand for a few seconds until combined. Add the flour and salt and, using the mixer's dough-hook attachment, mix on medium speed until the dough comes together, 3 to 5 minutes. (You can add a little more flour if the dough seems too sticky.) Let the dough rest in the bowl for 5 minutes, then continue mixing, sprinkling on more flour if necessary and stopping once or twice to scrape down the dough hook and the sides of the bowl, until the dough is fairly smooth, 3 to 5 minutes more.

On a well-floured surface, roll and tighten the dough into a ball. If you're freezing the dough, wrap the ball of dough tightly in plastic wrap and place it in the freezer; it will keep there for up to 1 month. If you're going to make the challah (or pletzel or cinnamon buns) right away, place the dough in a bowl that's lightly greased with oil or cooking spray, cover the bowl tightly with plastic wrap, and let the dough rest in a warm, draft-free area until roughly doubled in size, about 2 hours, before proceeding with the recipe.

recipe continues →

IF YOU'RE MAKING A PULLMAN LOAF, SHAPE THE DOUGH: Transfer the dough ball to a well-floured surface and press and stretch it into a roughly 10-by-8-inch rectangle. With the short edge of the rectangle facing you, start rolling the dough forward into a cylinder. Coat your hands with flour a few times if necessary to keep the dough from sticking to them. Tuck in any loose edges or ends so that you have a snug, even-sided loaf; transfer the rolled dough to a standard-size loaf pan that's greased with oil or cooking spray. Lightly grease the top of the loaf and cover the pan with plastic wrap; let the dough rest in the pan in a warm, draft-free area until it has risen roughly to the top edge of the pan, about 1½ hours.

IF YOU'RE MAKING A BRAIDED LOAF, SHAPE THE DOUGH: Transfer the dough ball to a well-floured surface and divide it into 3 equal portions. Working with 1 portion at a time (and using plenty of flour to keep the dough from sticking), use the flat of your hands to roll the dough portion into a narrow, roughly 12-inch-long strip that's slightly tapered at the ends and slightly fatter in the middle. Repeat with the remaining 2 dough portions so that you end up with 3 strips of roughly equal length.

Arrange 1 strip of dough perpendicular to the edge of the table in front of you, then arrange the other 2 strips at a 45-degree angle to the middle one, so that the far tips of each strip are just overlapping. Squish the overlapping tips together with your fingers so that they're well stuck together.

BRAID THE CHALLAH: Gently lift one of the outer strips, bring it over the middle strip, and lay it down alongside the other outer strip. Next, gently lift the other outer strip and bring it over the middle, laying it down alongside the opposite strip, gently tugging the strips taut so there aren't any gaps. Repeat this braiding process until you've reached the ends of the strips; pinch together the ends. Tuck both pinched ends of the braided strips under the loaf and transfer the loaf to a 10-by-15-inch baking sheet that's been greased with oil or cooking spray. Lightly grease the top of the loaf, cover it with plastic wrap, and let it rest in a warm, draft-free area for about 1½ hours.

When you're ready to bake, remove the plastic wrap and brush the top of the braided dough with the egg wash. Place the sesame seeds or poppy seeds on a plate, moisten your index finger in water, and press it into the seeds. Then press your finger onto the top surface of one of the braids; the seeds should come off onto the dough. Repeat so that each braided segment has a decorative patch of seeds on it.

BAKE THE CHALLAH: Preheat the oven to 350°F during the final rise.

Bake the challah for about 25 minutes, rotating the pan or tray 180 degrees halfway through cooking, until an instant-read thermometer inserted into the center of the bread reads 180°F. If you're making the Pullman loaf, let the bread rest for 5 minutes before unmolding it.

MAKES 1 PULLMAN OR BRAIDED LOAF

Keith Cohen
Owner, Orwasher's Bakery, New York City

A Bread-Maker's Journey

ORWASHER'S IS THE OLDEST BREAD BAKERY in New York City. When I bought the place, it was on its third generation and had been in the same spot on the Upper East Side since 1916, having survived economic turmoil and two World Wars, just making rye and pumpernickel and challah day after day. But it had sort of reached the end of its natural life span. It needed to be reinvented.

I wasn't entirely sure what I was doing, but I did have some history on my side. My grandfather and great-grandfather were both kosher butchers in Brooklyn, and I've loved working with my hands since I was a kid. I grew up in Bayside, Queens, and I was supposed to go into a white-collar profession—and not the kind of white collar on a baker's uniform—but I was more interested in cars than school. I had a 1971 Mustang and then a 1970 Trans Am; they were pieces of crap, but I learned how to change the brakes, change the springs, find my way around the engine. I was just a mechanical kind of guy, and early on, my dream was to go to Germany to learn how to fix Mercedeses and Audis.

Instead, after college, I ended up getting a job at a bakery, and lo and behold, baking scratched that same itch. The place was called Tribeca Oven, and I stayed there for fourteen years, learning every facet of the trade, from production to customer service to repairing equipment. I loved the physical mechanics and chemistry of bread-making. For me, it wasn't that different from customizing a car. You get a vision in your head of how the car, or loaf of bread, is going to look and feel and perform, and you realize that vision. In 2007, I decided it was time to go out on my own.

Taking over a place like Orwasher's, and figuring out how to rejuvenate it, was kind of a delicate dance. Its bread was great, and people had been buying it for a long time and had come to love it just as it was. But I knew it could be better. Still, I didn't want to change everything at once and disenfranchise all those longtime customers. So it took time, about two years, to really start making that transition from the old Orwasher's to the new. We kept the hundred-year-old brick oven the old owners had always used, but added another, more modern one, too. We also came up with proper written recipes, with exact, to-the-gram quantities and precise baking times and temperatures. The old Orwasher recipes had been passed down from father to son, with the assumption that everyone knew what a "pinch of salt" meant, but that wasn't going to work for us. Plus, I wanted to work with all-natural flours; I didn't want to have any bleached or bromated stuff. Natural flours have different absorption rates and required new recipes, new proportions. We also modified the rye starters, creating ones we could control better, and endlessly tweaked the fermentation times until we got them just right.

Even as I was working to update the bakery, I was constantly looking to the past. I wanted to replicate traditional old-world baking techniques. I tried to use refrigerators and retarders as little as possible, and I became really interested in older methods of natural fermentation. In 2008, I started experimenting with the ancient technique of making bread using the natural yeasts that grow on the skins of wine grapes. My friend Christopher Tracey at Channing Daughters Winery on Long Island gave me part of his Chardonnay and Cabernet harvest, and we used the grape yeasts to create natural starters. These starters are very robust. There's a difference in their yeast makeup, and the breads they make are totally distinctive, with gorgeous crusts. Orwasher's also used to make an old-school bread called corn rye, which I initially phased out, since only a handful of customers still asked for it. But now I'm working on reviving it. I want to make these old breads new again, for a new generation.

I also started using flour made from local grain. I'm a proud New Yorker, and this state used to grow a lot of wheat. In fact, there's a high probability that the first loaves that came out of the Orwasher's oven were made with New York State wheat. After an enormous amount of trial and error, I came up with what we call the "Ultimate" whole wheat bread. It has a great, light crumb structure—it's not a brick, like most whole wheats—and is 100 percent healthy whole New York wheat.

Years ago in Europe, bread tasted different from region to region because everyone had to use ingredients from within a few miles of where they lived, using airborne yeasts from each particular hillside or valley. The tastes of those foods bound people together. That's what I'm trying to do at Orwasher's: bring people together by making bread that tastes of a place.

KAISER, WECK & ONION ROLLS

Rae: The kaiser is the classic New York roll: sturdy, mild-tasting, and able to stand up to savory, flavorful fillings without overpowering them. It's what we use for our Smoked Mackerel Sandwich (page 131). Add a shower of caraway seeds and coarse salt, though, and it becomes something more intense: just right for the minimally seasoned roast beef in the classic sandwich called Beef on Weck (page 128). Then there's the onion roll, which we use at Mile End for our Ruth Wilensky sandwich (page 122); it's just a simple round roll sprinkled with our pletzel topping—so tasty that we sometimes eat these rolls all on their own.

FOR THE DOUGH:
- 1 large egg
- 1 tablespoon canola oil
- 4½ teaspoons sugar
- 1 teaspoon instant yeast
- ¾ cup lukewarm water
- 3 cups plus 2 tablespoons bread flour
- 1 teaspoon Diamond Crystal kosher salt
- 1 additional large egg, beaten, for the egg wash

ADDITIONAL INGREDIENTS FOR WECK ROLLS:
- Caraway seeds
- Coarse salt

ADDITIONAL INGREDIENTS FOR ONION ROLLS:
- Pletzel topping (refer to the "Make the Pletzel Topping" section of the Pletzel recipe on page 184)

MAKE THE DOUGH: In the bowl of a stand mixer, hand-whisk the egg, oil, sugar, yeast, and water until thoroughly combined, about 10 seconds. Add the flour and salt and, using the mixer's dough-hook attachment, start mixing on medium speed until the dough comes together and pulls away cleanly from the side of the bowl. Let the dough rest in the bowl for 5 minutes. Mix again on medium speed until the dough is smooth and uniform in texture, about 5 minutes more.

Transfer the dough to a large bowl that's lightly greased with oil. Cover the bowl with plastic wrap and let the dough rest in a warm, draft-free area until roughly doubled in size, about 1 hour.

Transfer the dough to a floured surface and punch it down to get any air bubbles out. Return the dough to the bowl, cover it in plastic wrap, and refrigerate overnight.

Unwrap the dough and divide it into 6 equal-size pieces. **1.** Shape each of the dough pieces into a ball; let the dough balls rest, covered in plastic wrap, for 20 minutes. If you're making onion rolls, gently flatten the rolls to about ½-inch thickness and prepare for baking. **2.** Next, working on a lightly floured surface with one dough ball at a time, use your hands to roll the dough into a thin, roughly 18-inch-long strip. Set aside, covered by a damp towel, and repeat with the remaining dough. **3-4.** Starting with the first piece of dough, tie a basic square knot: Make a loop, then grip the segment of the strip that's laying on top of the other one and pull it under and through the loop. **5-6.** Next, take the two ends and pass them through the loop again, at approximately 2 and 10 o'clock. Repeat with the remaining dough.

Line a light-colored 10-by-15-inch baking sheet with parchment paper and grease it with oil or cooking spray; place the rolls on the sheet, lightly grease the tops of the rolls, cover them with plastic wrap, and let them rest in a warm, draft-free area for 1 hour.

BAKE THE ROLLS: Preheat the oven to 425°F.

Uncover the rolls and brush them with the egg wash.

IF YOU'RE MAKING WECK ROLLS: Sprinkle 1 teaspoon each of caraway seeds and coarse salt on each roll before baking.

IF YOU'RE MAKING ONION ROLLS: Sprinkle pletzel topping generously over the rolls, tamping into the dough as you go.

Bake the rolls, rotating the tray 180 degrees halfway through cooking, until they're light golden brown, 15 to 20 minutes.

MAKES 6

HOW TO SHAPE A KAISER ROLL

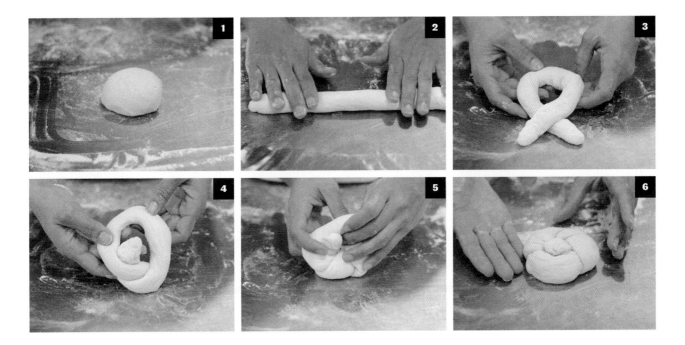

PLETZEL

Noah: Rae and I didn't know much about this traditional Jewish bread before opening Mile End, and when I asked my grandfather about it, he just said, "It's what you serve with chopped liver!" So that's what we do. We make ours as a flatbread using our challah dough, and then we cut the pletzel into triangles. In New York and even in Montreal, I've seen places serving onion rolls and calling them pletzel, and other places serving a super-thin, matzo-like pletzel. Ours is more like a focaccia, with a nice chew and a savory bite.

- 1 full portion Challah dough (follow the Challah recipe on page 177 through the end of the "Make the Dough" section)
- 1 large egg, beaten, for the egg wash
- 1 cup dried minced onion
- ¼ cup poppy seeds
- 2 tablespoons Diamond Crystal kosher salt
- ½ cup lukewarm water

Place the challah dough on a rimmed 10-by-15-inch baking sheet and use your hands and fingertips to flatten the dough so that it covers the sheet and has an even thickness all over. (If the dough starts to get stiff, just leave it alone for a few minutes to let it loosen up before continuing to press and flatten it.) Use a fork to lightly dimple the dough all over. Brush the dough generously with the egg wash.

MAKE THE PLETZEL TOPPING: Mix the dried onion, poppy seeds, salt, and lukewarm water in a bowl and let the mixture sit for 15 minutes. Mix it again briefly with your hand, and then sprinkle the topping evenly, and generously, over the dough (you might have a little topping left over).

BAKE THE PLETZEL: Preheat the oven to 350°F.

Bake for 15 to 20 minutes, rotating the tray 90 degrees every few minutes until the pletzel is golden brown all over. Let the pletzel cool before cutting.

MAKES 1 SHEET

MATZO

Rae: You'd think more people would make their own matzo instead of buying it in a box—the recipe couldn't be simpler, and come on, it's the star of the Passover story. I use our homemade matzo instead of crackers all the time for snacks and hors d'oeuvres. How many pieces of matzo you get from this recipe will depend on how practiced you are at rolling and trimming the dough.

- 4¼ cups sifted all-purpose flour, plus more as needed
- 1 teaspoon Diamond Crystal kosher salt, plus more to top the matzo (optional)
- 2 tablespoons canola oil
- ¾ cup plus 1 tablespoon warm water

Preheat the oven to 500°F and place a pizza stone (ideally) or a 10-by-15-inch baking sheet on the bottom rack.

In a large bowl, mix together all the ingredients until they come together to form a dough. If the dough is sticky, add a bit more flour.

Divide the dough into 8 pieces. Flatten a piece slightly and pass it repeatedly through a pasta maker, reducing the thickness each time until you reach the minimum setting. (Or you can simply roll the dough as thinly as possible with a rolling pin.) Repeat with the remaining dough pieces.

Trim the flattened dough pieces so that they will fit snugly onto the pizza stone or baking sheet. Use a fork to prick holes in the surface of the dough. For salted matzo, brush or spray the dough surface lightly with water and sprinkle with salt.

Carefully slide the pieces of dough onto the pizza stone or baking sheet. Bake until the surface of the matzo is golden brown and bubbly, 30 seconds or so. Using tongs, carefully flip the matzo pieces and continue to bake until the other side is browned and lightly blistered. (Keep careful, constant watch to keep the matzo from burning; the exact cooking time will vary from oven to oven, and will get a little longer with each subsequent batch.)

MAKES ABOUT 8 LARGE SHEETS

Honey Cake

Cakes, Cookies & Sweets

CHEESECAKE

Rae: New York Jews have loved cheesecake for ages, especially around Shavuot (when you're supposed to eat dairy). The key is very good-quality cream cheese; we use Ben's, a real cultured cream cheese made in New York.

FOR THE CRUST:

- 2 cups crushed graham crackers (about 12 crackers)
- 2 teaspoons Diamond Crystal kosher salt
- ¼ cup sugar
- ½ cup (1 stick) unsalted butter, melted

FOR THE FILLING:

- 1¼ pounds cream cheese, at room temperature
- ¼ cup sour cream
- ¾ cup sugar
- 1½ teaspoons Diamond Crystal kosher salt
- 3 large eggs
- 1 large egg yolk
- Juice of ½ lemon
- 1 tablespoon vanilla extract

MAKE THE CRUST: Mix the graham-cracker crumbs, salt, sugar, and butter in a large bowl until the ingredients are thoroughly combined and the mixture has the consistency of wet sand.

MAKE THE FILLING: In the bowl of a stand mixer, using a paddle attachment, combine the cream cheese, sour cream, sugar, and salt and mix on medium speed, stopping once or twice to scrape down the sides as necessary, until the sugar is thoroughly incorporated, about 3 minutes.

Whisk together the eggs, egg yolk, lemon juice, and vanilla in a separate bowl and pour the egg mixture in a slow, steady stream into the bowl of the stand mixer while the mixer is running. After a few seconds, stop the mixer and scrape the sides and bottom of the bowl. Mix on medium-high speed until the mixture is totally smooth and uniform in appearance, about 1 minute, stopping the mixer as needed to scrape the sides and bottom of the bowl.

recipe continues →

BAKE THE CHEESECAKE: Preheat the oven to 350°F.

Grease a 12-inch cake pan generously with oil or cooking spray and line the pan with a circle of parchment paper trimmed to fit snugly in the bottom of the pan; grease the top of the parchment paper as well. Spread the graham-cracker mixture evenly over the bottom of the pan, making sure there aren't any overly thick or thin patches. Use the flat of your hand and your fingertips to press down on the crust, working all the way to the edges of the pan. Bake the crust on its own for about 10 minutes; let it cool for at least 30 minutes.

Raise the oven temperature to 500°F. Pour the filling into the prepared crust and set the cake pan in the middle of a baking dish; place the baking dish and cake pan in the oven and pour enough hot water into the baking dish to reach about a third of the way up the sides of the cake pan. Bake until the top of the cake has just started to brown, 5 to 10 minutes (monitor the cake closely, and rotate the baking dish if browning is uneven).

Reduce the oven temperature to 225°F and bake for about 1 hour, until a thermometer inserted in the center of the cake reads 150°F, taking care to rotate the dish 180 degrees halfway through cooking. Remove the baking dish and pan from the oven, taking care not to slosh any water left in the dish. Set the cake pan on a rack to cool. Refrigerate the cake for at least 3 hours before inverting it onto a plate, unmolding it, and carefully inverting it again onto a serving plate so that the crust side is down.

TIP: *You can find Ben's at any of the Murray's Cheese Shops or Fairway Markets in New York City; they also ship across the country.*

SERVES 10 TO 12

COMPOTE

Noah: I always wanted Mile End's food to have a strong seasonal feel. One way we achieve that is with the house-made fruit compotes that accompany our Cheesecake (page 191) and our Blintzes (page 110), and also breakfast dishes like our Bagelach (page 113) and Twice-Baked Challah (page 116). The tart apple-cranberry-walnut version is great for fall and winter, whereas the sweeter apricot-vanilla one evokes spring and summer. The fig and honey compote is just right for late summer and early fall—nothing is better with Olive Oil Cake (page 195). All of these compotes keep in the refrigerator for weeks, so make a bigger batch if you want. They're also nice on a piece of toast with some almond butter.

Apple Cranberry Walnut Compote

- 1 cup maple syrup
- 4 Braeburn, Fuji, or other crisp apples, peeled, cored, and sliced
- 1 cup dried cranberries
- ¾ cup walnut pieces
  Juice of 1 lemon
- 1 teaspoon Diamond Crystal kosher salt
- ½ cup (1 stick) unsalted butter

Pour the maple syrup into a medium saucepan over medium heat. Bring to a simmer and cook until reduced by half. Add the apples, cranberries, walnuts, and lemon juice and continue to simmer for another 20 minutes. Add the salt and butter and stir to combine. Let the compote cool before serving.

SERVES 4

Apricot Vanilla Compote

- ½ cup (1 stick) unsalted butter
- ½ cup sugar
- 1 vanilla bean, split
- 12 fresh apricots, quartered
  Pinch of Diamond Crystal kosher salt
  Toasted pistachios or almonds, for topping (optional)

Melt the butter in a saucepan over medium heat, then add the sugar and vanilla bean and cook for 3 minutes. Add the apricots and salt and cook for another minute. Let the compote cool, remove the vanilla bean, and serve. Top with toasted pistachios or almonds, if you like.

SERVES 4

Fig and Honey Compote

- 1 cup honey
  Juice and zest of 1 lemon
- 1 sprig of thyme
- 2 pints fresh Mission or Turkish figs, cut in half
- 1 teaspoon Diamond Crystal kosher salt
- ¼ cup extra-virgin olive oil

Pour the honey into a large saucepan over high heat and cook until it's caramelized, about 5 minutes. Add the lemon juice, thyme, and figs and stir to combine. Turn off the heat, then add the salt, olive oil, and lemon zest; stir to combine. Let the compote cool before serving.

SERVES 4

FLOURLESS CHOCOLATE CAKE

Noah: When I was a kid, my grandmother used to call me a chocoholic, but I always thought she was saying "chocolate olive." It didn't really matter. She had me at "chocolate." Though the recipe calls for butter, this ridiculously rich cake, which we came up with as a Passover Seder dessert, was inspired by the fudgy nondairy brownies my nana used to make on Friday nights for her chocolate olive.

 8 large eggs, chilled
 ½ cup sugar
 1 cup (2 sticks) unsalted butter
 1 pound bittersweet chocolate, chopped into fairly uniform pieces
 1 tablespoon dehydrated coffee
  Powdered sugar, flake salt, and fresh raspberries (optional), for serving

Preheat the oven to 325°F. Combine the eggs and sugar in the bowl of a stand mixer and mix with a whisk attachment on medium speed for about 1 minute; then increase the speed to high and continue to mix until completely smooth, about 5 minutes more.

Place the butter and chocolate in a double boiler over simmering water, stirring occasionally until they've melted, then add the coffee. Remove the double boiler from the heat.

Scrape the butter-chocolate mixture into a large bowl, then add the egg mixture in 3 equal portions: Pour the first portion in and stir with a spatula until the ingredients are incorporated; add the other 2 portions more slowly, folding the egg mixture into the butter-chocolate mixture more gently until no streaking is visible and the ingredients have melded together.

Line a 12-inch round cake pan with a circle of parchment paper trimmed to fit snugly in the bottom of the pan; grease the lined pan with a light film of oil or cooking spray. Pour the batter into the cake pan and set the pan in the middle of a baking dish; place the baking dish and cake pan in the oven and pour enough hot water into the baking dish to reach about a third of the way up the sides of the cake pan. Bake, rotating the cake pan 180 degrees halfway through cooking, until an instant-read thermometer inserted into the center reads 140°F, or a toothpick inserted and removed comes out clean, about 15 to 20 minutes.

Remove the cake and its baking-dish bath from the oven, taking care not to slosh any water left in the dish. Set the cake pan on a rack to cool, then run a small knife around the outside of the pan to loosen the cake from the sides. Invert it onto a plate, removing the parchment. Refrigerate the cake for at least 3 hours or overnight to set. Let the cake come to room temperature; dust it with powdered sugar and sprinkle it with a pinch of coarse salt. Serve with fresh raspberries, if you like.

SERVES 8 TO 10

OLIVE OIL CAKE

Rae: This dessert isn't a traditional Jewish thing, or even a Montreal thing. It's a Brooklyn thing—it's based on cakes you'll find at some of the old Italian bakeries in Carroll Gardens, near our deli. This cake is perfect for Hanukkah, with oil being central to the story of the holiday. What's more, it's still perfectly good for up to a week after you've made it.

3 large eggs
Zest of 1 lemon
3 cups sugar
1½ cups pomace olive oil (or substitute 1 cup canola oil and ½ cup regular olive oil)
1½ cups whole milk
2½ cups all-purpose flour
½ teaspoon baking powder
½ teaspoon baking soda
1 teaspoon Diamond Crystal kosher salt
Powdered sugar, extra-virgin olive oil, fresh berries, and crème fraîche (optional), for serving

Preheat the oven to 350°F. Place the eggs and lemon zest in the bowl of a stand mixer and mix on medium speed for a few seconds. While the mixer is running, add 1¼ cups of the sugar and mix until it's dissolved, 10 to 15 seconds more. Keep the mixer running and add the oil in a slow, steady stream. Continue mixing for another minute, and then add the milk in a slow, steady stream. Mix for another few seconds.

Stop the mixer and add the flour, baking powder, baking soda, salt, and remaining 1¾ cups of sugar to the bowl; mix on low speed for a few seconds to bring the ingredients together, then on medium speed for about 3 minutes, stopping a few times to scrape down the sides of the bowl, until you have a smooth and fairly thin batter.

Line a 12-inch round cake pan with a circle of parchment paper trimmed to fit snugly in the bottom of the pan; grease the lined pan with a light film of oil or cooking spray.

Pour the batter into the pan and bake, rotating the pan 180 degrees halfway through cooking, until the top has split and become a deep golden brown and an instant-read thermometer inserted into the center of the cake reads 200°F, about 35 minutes (closer to 40 minutes if you're using a Bundt pan). Let the cake cool, and then turn it out onto a serving plate. Garnish with a dusting of powdered sugar and a drizzle of good extra-virgin olive oil, and serve with fresh berries and crème fraîche, if you like.

SERVES 8 TO 10

Joan Nathan

Best-selling author and Jewish-cooking maven,
at Mile End with Noah

Wisdom from My Jewish Kitchen

My favorite cookbooks:
Oh, so many! For old Jewish recipes, the 1947 Community Cookbook from Woonsocket, Rhode Island. For cooking, I love *The Silver Palate*, Julia Child's *Mastering the Art of French Cooking*, and all of Maida Heatter's, Madeleine Kamman's, and Marcella Hazan's books. Plus my own, of course! I probably use those the most.

A dish that works for every holiday:
Chicken soup with matzo balls. Who doesn't love that?

The biggest mistake I've made in the kitchen:
When I was very young, living in a tiny apartment in New York City, with absolutely no money, I threw a dessert party during Pasover. I decided to bake a delicious, delicate carrot torte. Unfortunately, when we cut into it, out ran a gooey mess. I thought that I had whipped the egg whites into stiff peaks, but I guess not!

A great piece of advice for aspiring cooks:
Work your way through a favorite but very detailed cookbook. If you're interested in baking, Peter Reinhart's bread book is a good place to start. Julia Child is always a wonderful teacher. They both write very clear recipes that will guide you through the process step by step. There are also lots of great cooking shows on television. It always helps to have someone to watch.

An easy but delicious dessert:
I love to end dinner with tortes. They're so easy—once you master stiff peaks! My absolute favorite is a coconut Cointreau torte that I learned from my Moroccan cleaning lady when I was living in Israel many years ago.

My last meal:
I'd start with a salmon ceviche with avocado, then white truffle pasta from Florence, a dish you can only get about a month out of the year. Next would be chicken with black truffles, and I'd finish with a puckery, tart lemon tart.

My biggest achievement:
My children, of course!

Essential kitchen equipment:
I like doing things the old-fashioned way. I would be in trouble without my dough cutter, whisk, spider strainer, good set of knives, tongs, flexible rubber spatulas, and lots of wooden spoons.

I couldn't live without:
Preserved lemons.

My cooking process:
Compared to many writers I know, I'd say my style is relaxed and flexible. But there's also an intensity to it. I want everything to turn out deliciously!

A secret ingredient:
I always add fresh grated ginger to my matzo balls. It adds a gentle kick.

An early cooking memory:
I first appreciated the power of food when I was working for Teddy Kollek, the mayor of Jerusalem. We were visiting a Palestinian village, and there was a great deal of tension in the air over a road that the villagers wanted built. Not to mention the political situation. Then we sat down to break bread over *musakhan*, still my favorite chicken dish in the world, and all the tension melted away. It was delicious, and the villagers got their road.

The best cooking tip I've ever received:
My mother always said to prepare in advance. Not just to cook in advance but, more important, to make lists. And lists and lists.

My ideal cooking situation:
Cooking in my own kitchen with somebody else to clean up!

HONEY CAKE

Noah: We adapted this recipe from a version by baker extraordinaire Marcy Goldman, who used to live down the street from my parents in Montreal. It's actually based on an old gingerbread recipe.

1 cup orange juice
1 cup honey, plus more for drizzling
½ teaspoon baking soda
3 large eggs, at room temperature
1 cup (packed) light brown sugar
1 cup sugar
¾ cup canola oil
2 cups all-purpose flour

1½ teaspoons baking powder
¼ teaspoon ground cloves
1 tablespoon ground cinnamon
½ teaspoon ground nutmeg
1 teaspoon Diamond Crystal kosher salt
Toasted almonds (optional)
Powdered sugar (optional)
Crème fraîche (optional), for serving

Preheat the oven to 350°F. Combine the orange juice and honey in a large saucepan. Place it over medium-low heat, bring it to a simmer, and simmer until the liquids have come together and you can no longer feel any honey sticking to the bottom of the pan, about 5 minutes. Remove the pan from the heat and add the baking soda; stir to combine, then set the pan aside.

In a large bowl, combine the eggs and sugars and whisk vigorously until smooth. Then add the oil and whisk until the mixture is completely emulsified and smooth. Pour the reserved orange-juice mixture into the egg mixture and whisk for a few seconds to combine.

In another large bowl, combine the flour, baking powder, cloves, cinnamon, nutmeg, and salt; mix together with a spatula. Pour the liquid mixture into the dry ingredients and whisk, scraping down the sides with a spatula, until any lumps are eliminated, 10 to 15 seconds.

Grease a Bundt pan with oil or cooking spray and dust the pan liberally with flour, tapping out any excess. Pour the batter into the pan and bake on the middle rack of the oven until the surface of the cake starts turning a dark golden brown, about 15 minutes. Rotate the pan 180 degrees and tent it lightly with aluminum foil. Continue baking until a thermometer inserted into the center of the cake reads 200°F, another 20 to 25 minutes. Cool the cake completely on a wire rack. Invert it onto a serving plate and drizzle it with honey. Top with toasted almonds and powdered sugar, and serve with crème fraîche, if you like.

SERVES 8 TO 10

CARROT CAKE

Noah: This is the ultimate carrot cake—it's luscious and brings out the natural sweetness of the carrots. When I was a kid, I loved the cream cheese frosting.

FOR THE CAKE:

- 3 large eggs
- 1½ cups sugar
- ½ cup (packed) light brown sugar
- 1½ cups vegetable oil
- 1 pound large carrots, peeled and grated
- 2½ cups all-purpose flour
- 1¼ teaspoons baking powder
- 1 teaspoon baking soda
- ½ tablespoon ground cinnamon
- ½ teaspoon ground nutmeg
  Pinch of ground cloves
- 1 teaspoon Diamond Crystal kosher salt

FOR THE FROSTING:

- 1 pound cream cheese, at room temperature
- ½ cup powdered sugar
  Pinch of Diamond Crystal kosher salt
- ¼ cup sour cream
- 1 teaspoon vanilla extract
  Chopped walnuts (optional), for garnish

MAKE THE CAKE: Preheat the oven to 350°F and grease a 12-inch cake pan with oil or cooking spray.

In the bowl of a food processor, combine the eggs and sugars and process until the sugars dissolve, about 20 seconds. Add the oil in a slow, steady stream while the processor is running; continue processing until the mixture is emulsified, 10 to 15 seconds. Add the grated carrots, and pulse 5 or 6 times, until they're incorporated.

Pour the egg mixture into a large bowl and add the flour, baking powder, baking soda, cinnamon, nutmeg, cloves, and salt. Fold the ingredients together using a spatula, continuing to mix until the batter is smooth and no streaks appear (don't worry about overmixing).

Pour the batter into the prepared pan. Bake, rotating the pan 180 degrees halfway through cooking, until the cake is golden brown and a toothpick inserted into the middle comes out clean, about 30 minutes. Transfer to a wire rack to cool.

MAKE THE FROSTING: Combine all the frosting ingredients, except the walnuts, in the bowl of a stand mixer fitted with the whisk attachment and mix on medium-high speed until the mixture is light and airy, 4 to 5 minutes.

Invert the cooled cake onto a plate and spread the frosting over the top and along the sides. Sprinkle with chopped walnuts, if you like.

SERVES 8 TO 10

HAMANTASCHEN

Rae: We wanted to come up with a version of this Purim pastry that was light and crumbly but not dry, and these really fit the bill. At Mile End we make the three classic kinds: apricot, poppy seed, and prune. If you want to make a mixed batch, just make all three fillings, using a third of the amount of each of the filling ingredients called for below. Mile End's baker, Rich Maggi, swears by his tortilla press for flattening the dough, though a rolling pin will also do the trick.

FOR THE DOUGH:
- 4 cups all-purpose flour
- 1 teaspoon baking powder
- 2 teaspoons Diamond Crystal kosher salt
- Zest of 1 lemon
- 4 large eggs
- 1 cup sugar
- 1 cup canola oil
- ¼ cup lukewarm water

FOR THE POPPY-SEED FILLING:
- 1 cup poppy seeds
- 1½ cups dark raisins
- 1½ cups golden raisins
- ½ teaspoon ground cloves
- ½ teaspoon Diamond Crystal kosher salt
- ½ teaspoon ground cinnamon
- 1 cup sugar
- 2 cups water

FOR THE APRICOT OR PRUNE FILLING:
- 2 cups dried apricots or dried prunes
- 1 cup sugar
- 1 cup water

MAKE THE DOUGH: Combine the flour, baking powder, salt, and lemon zest in a large bowl and mix them together with your hands until thoroughly combined. In a separate bowl, whisk the eggs, sugar, and oil together vigorously until thoroughly combined. Pour the egg mixture into the dry ingredients and mix them together with your hands for 10 to 15 seconds. Add the water and continue mixing with your hands until the dough comes together, another 30 seconds or so.

Scrape the dough onto a floured surface, adding a little more flour if the dough is too sticky. Use your hand to flatten the dough slightly into a thick disk, and wrap the disk very snugly in aluminum foil. Refrigerate until the dough is firmly set, about 3 hours.

recipe continues ➔

MAKE THE APRICOT OR PRUNE FILLING: Combine all the filling ingredients in a medium saucepan and bring them to a boil over medium-high heat; reduce the heat and simmer for 5 minutes. Set the mixture aside until it is just cool enough to handle, then transfer it to the bowl of a food processor and process until smooth. Refrigerate the filling until it's completely cooled before using.

MAKE THE POPPY-SEED FILLING: Combine all the filling ingredients in a medium saucepan and bring to a boil over medium-high heat; reduce the heat and simmer until the mixture has reduced somewhat, 15 to 20 minutes. Set the mixture aside until it is just cool enough to handle, then transfer it to a food processor and process until the poppy seeds have broken down and are thoroughly incorporated, 5 to 6 minutes. Refrigerate the filling until it's completely cooled before using.

SHAPE, FILL, AND BAKE THE COOKIES: Remove the dough from the refrigerator (it will look and feel quite oily) and transfer it to a floured surface. **1-2.** Tear off a small piece of dough and roll it between your hands into a ball roughly the size of a Ping-Pong ball; use your hand to flatten the ball into a thick disk. Repeat with the remaining dough to make roughly 28 disks and hold them in the refrigerator. **3-4.** Then, pull one disk out at a time and place it onto a sheet of floured parchment paper. Fold the edge of the paper over the top of the disk, and use a tortilla press or rolling pin to flatten the dough until it's roughly doubled in width. Using the same sheet of parchment and adding flour as needed, repeat with the remaining dough pieces. **5.** Working with 1 flattened piece of dough at a time, dollop a heaping tablespoon of the filling of your choice in the center of the dough. **6.** Then gently fold 1 edge of the dough over the side (but not over the top) of the filling and press the edge slightly against the filling so it stays in place. **7.** Next, bring up a second edge the same way. **8.** Finally, bring up the third edge and pinch the 3 seams together, creating a triangular pastry with a little of the filling still exposed at the top. Transfer it to a 10-by-15-inch baking sheet that's lined with parchment paper and greased with oil or cooking spray (use a bench knife or a metal spatula to gently scrape the bottom of the filled cookie off the work surface, if necessary). Repeat with the remaining dough and filling. Cover the filled cookies with plastic wrap and refrigerate them for about 30 minutes.

Preheat the oven to 350°F. Remove the plastic wrap and bake the cookies, rotating the tray halfway through baking, until golden brown, 10 to 15 minutes.

MAKES ABOUT 28 COOKIES

HAMANTASCHEN, STEP BY STEP

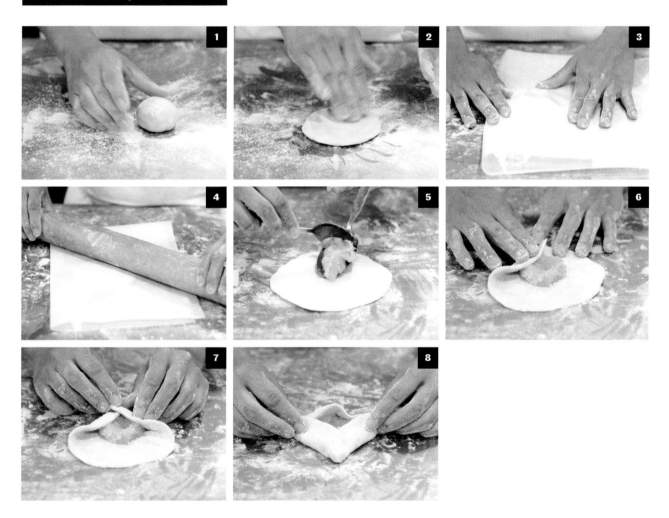

MANDELBROT

Noah: When I was growing up, mandelbrot—aka the Jewish biscotti—were the most prized treat on my family's Friday-night cookie plate. Nana Lee always baked extra so we could snack on them throughout the week. At Mile End they're a hit at all times of the day: crunchy, nutty, just sweet enough, and perfect with coffee.

4	ounces almond paste, broken into small chunks
1	cup sugar
½	cup (1 stick) unsalted butter, at room temperature
½	cup sliced almonds
2	large eggs, beaten
1	teaspoon vanilla extract
1	teaspoon almond extract
2	cups all-purpose flour
¼	teaspoon ground cinnamon
½	teaspoon baking powder
¼	teaspoon baking soda
½	cup whole blanched almonds
1	teaspoon Diamond Crystal kosher salt
1	additional large egg, beaten, for the egg wash
	Coarse decorative sugar, for sprinkling

Preheat the oven to 350°F. Line a 10-by-15-inch baking sheet with parchment paper and grease the paper with oil or cooking spray.

Combine the almond paste, sugar, butter, and sliced almonds in the bowl of a stand mixer fitted with the paddle attachment. Mix on medium speed until the mixture has a uniform, pastelike consistency and is light and aerated, 3 to 4 minutes.

Whisk together the two eggs and the vanilla and almond extracts in a separate bowl. Restart the mixer on medium-high speed and add the egg mixture to the creamed-sugar mixture while the mixer is running. Mix for a few seconds, and scrape down the sides of the bowl.

Add the flour, cinnamon, baking powder, baking soda, almonds, and salt to the mixer bowl and mix on low speed just until the dough comes together, 15 to 20 seconds. Scrape the paddle and the sides and bottom of the bowl. Place the bowl in the refrigerator for at least 2 hours or overnight to let the dough firm up.

Place the chilled dough—it should have a clay-like consistency—on a generously floured work surface and sprinkle flour over the top of the dough. Roll the dough into a roughly 12-inch-long cylinder and gently pat the top and sides flat.

Transfer the dough to the prepared baking sheet, brush the top and sides with the egg wash, and sprinkle with decorative sugar.

Bake the dough, rotating the sheet 180 degrees halfway through cooking, until it has roughly doubled in size, 20 to 25 minutes. Remove it from the oven and let it cool briefly, then put the sheet into the refrigerator for at least 3 hours or overnight so the baked dough will firm up and be easy to slice.

Preheat the oven to 300°F. Using a bread knife, slice the baked dough crosswise into ½-inch-thick pieces and transfer them to a baking sheet. (Discard the uneven end pieces, or let them air-dry for a day or so and then crumble them up to make a delicious ice cream topping.) Bake the mandelbrot on the center rack of the oven for about 20 minutes, rotating the tray 180 degrees about halfway through baking, until they're golden at the edges.

MAKES ABOUT 24 PIECES

Jelly Doughnuts

JELLY DOUGHNUTS

Rae: Jelly- and custard-filled doughnuts, called *sufganiyot* in Hebrew, are a big deal around Hanukkah in Israel. The ones we make are dainty little beauties filled with our house-made concord grape jelly.

FOR THE DOUGHNUTS:
- 4 tablespoons instant yeast
- 1 cup lukewarm water
- ½ cup sugar
- 4 eggs
- ¼ cup (½ stick) unsalted butter
- 1 teaspoon ground nutmeg
- 5 cups all-purpose flour
- 4 teaspoon Diamond Crystal kosher salt
- Canola oil
- 1 recipe Concord Grape Jelly (page 80)

FOR FINISHING:
- Powdered sugar
- Coarse salt

MAKE THE DOUGHNUTS: Add the first 6 doughnut ingredients to a large bowl and stir to combine. Add the flour and salt and stir (or mix with your hands) until the dough comes together (it will still be wet and sticky).

On a well-floured surface, knead and shape the dough into a thick disk; transfer it to a bowl that's greased with oil or cooking spray and let it rest in a warm, draft-free area for 1 hour.

On a well-floured surface, flatten the dough and roll it out into a ¼-inch-thick disk. Use a 2-inch round cookie cutter to cut out as many circles of dough as you can. Transfer the circles to a 10-by-15-inch baking sheet that's lined with parchment paper and greased with oil. Collect the dough trimmings and form them into another ball; roll it into another ¼-inch-thick disk, cut out more doughnuts, and transfer them to the baking sheet. Repeat with the remaining dough.

Let the dough circles rest in a warm, draft-free area for ½ hour. Then heat about 1 inch of oil in a high-sided skillet over medium-high heat until very hot but not smoking (365 to 375°F). Working in batches, fry the doughnuts until they're golden brown on one side, then flip them and finish frying, about 3 minutes total. Transfer the doughnuts to a paper towel to drain.

FILL AND FINISH: Transfer some of the filling to a pastry bag or to a zip-top bag with a small hole cut from one corner. When the doughnuts have cooled completely, use a small knife to gently burrow from the side of the doughnut to the center. Insert the tip of the bag into the opening and pipe in as much filling as possible. Repeat with the remaining doughnuts and filling. Dust the doughnuts generously with powdered sugar, and sprinkle each with a small pinch of coarse salt.

TIP: *Instead of using a thermometer to measure the oil temperature, you can test it by throwing in a cube of dry old bread. When it fries to golden brown in about a minute, the oil is the right temperature.*

MAKES 24

RUGELACH

Rae: This recipe has instructions for making three different fillings: cherry-almond, chocolate-hazelnut, and apricot; the dough and the shaping and baking instructions are the same for all of them. So pick your favorite filling, or do a mixed batch by making all three fillings and using a third of each amount of the filling ingredients called for below. We're always experimenting with new flavor combinations, so once you get the basics down, have fun mixing and matching. You can use this dough for the Apple Turnovers (page 111) and Bagelach (page 113), too.

FOR THE DOUGH:
- 2 cups (4 sticks) unsalted butter, cut into tablespoon-size pats
- 4 cups all-purpose flour
- 1 tablespoon Diamond Crystal kosher salt
- 1 pound cream cheese, chilled
- ¼ cup sour cream

FOR THE CHERRY-ALMOND FILLING:
- 2 cups dried tart cherries
- 1 cup sugar
- 1 cup water
- Pinch of Diamond Crystal kosher salt
- 1 teaspoon almond extract
- 1½ cups blanched and lightly toasted almonds

FOR THE CHOCOLATE-HAZELNUT FILLING:
- 2 cups coarsely chopped bittersweet chocolate
- 1 cup hazelnuts
- ½ cup (1 stick) unsalted butter
- ¼ cup all-purpose flour
- ½ cup sugar
- 1 tablespoon Diamond Crystal kosher salt

FOR THE APRICOT FILLING:
- 1 recipe apricot filling for Hamantaschen (page 201)

FOR FINISHING:
- Decorative coarse sugar, for sprinkling
- 1 large egg, beaten, for the egg wash

MAKE THE DOUGH: Combine the butter and flour in the bowl of a food processor and process until the chunks of butter are broken up and the mixture has taken on the consistency of wet sand, about 30 seconds.

Transfer the butter-flour mixture to a large mixing bowl and add the salt, cream cheese, and sour cream. Mix the ingredients together vigorously with your hands, breaking up the cream cheese and working it into the flour with your fingers until the mixture is crumbly and only pea-size chunks of the cream cheese remain.

Turn out the dough onto a sheet of aluminum foil, press it down slightly into a thick disk, and wrap it very tightly in the foil. Refrigerate it for at least 20 minutes or overnight. Meanwhile, make the filling.

recipe continues →

MAKE THE CHERRY-ALMOND FILLING: Combine the cherries, sugar, water, and salt in a medium saucepan and bring to a boil over medium-high heat; reduce the heat and simmer until syrupy, about 5 minutes. Remove from the heat and add the almond extract. Let the mixture rest until it's cool enough to handle. Place the almonds in the bowl of a food processor and process until crushed, about 10 seconds. Transfer the almonds to a bowl and add the reserved cherry mixture to the food processor; process until the mixture has a jamlike consistency, scraping down the sides of the machine as necessary. Add the almonds back in and process for a few seconds, until all the ingredients are thoroughly combined. The filling can be stored in the freezer for up to 2 months.

MAKE THE CHOCOLATE-HAZELNUT FILLING: Combine all the filling ingredients in the bowl of a food processor and process until crumbly. The filling can be stored in the freezer for up to 2 months.

MAKE THE APRICOT FILLING: Follow the instructions for the apricot filling for Hamantaschen (page 201). The filling can be stored in the freezer for up to 2 months.

SHAPE, FILL, AND BAKE THE RUGELACH: Preheat the oven to 350°F. Line a 10-by-15-inch baking sheet with parchment paper, grease it with oil or cooking spray, and sprinkle it with a small handful of decorative sugar.

Unwrap the dough and divide it into 2 equal-size portions. On a well-floured surface, press and work one of the dough portions into a ball, then press the ball into a disk that's about ¾ inch thick. The dough will be very firm at first and may crack around the edges, so keep working it and bringing the cracks together until you have a smooth-sided disk, adding more flour as needed to keep your hands from sticking to the dough.

Roll out the dough into a 10- to 12-inch circle of even thickness. Fold the circle into a half moon and use a knife or dough cutter to trim away any uneven or protruding edges, then unfold the dough so it's a circle again.

If you're using the chocolate-hazelnut filling, brush a little of the egg wash over the dough. Use a spatula to spread a heaping cup of the filling of your choice evenly over the dough. Then use a dough cutter or pizza cutter to cut the circle into 16 equal-size wedges, just as you would a pizza.

Then, working with one wedge at a time, roll a wedge up to make the rugelach, starting with the wide end and rolling toward the pointy end. Transfer the rugelach to the prepared baking sheet. Repeat with the remaining dough and filling.

Brush the tops of the rugelach with the egg wash, sprinkle lightly with more decorative sugar, and bake, rotating the tray 180 degrees halfway through cooking, until the pastries are light golden brown, 15 to 20 minutes.

MAKES 32

HOLIDAY ENTERTAINING MENUS

Freddie Roman, the creator and star of *Catskills on Broadway*, once said: *"The Jewish holidays are never on time. They're always either early or late."* Because they're determined by the lunar calendar, the Jewish holidays never fall at exactly the same time from year to year. Nevertheless, with each season comes a significant holiday, and food is always at the epicenter of that observance. Some gather each Friday to celebrate Shabbat, while others get together only for the major moments of the High Holidays in the fall, Hanukkah in the winter, and Passover in the spring. We hope that the recipes in this book become part of your everyday repertoire, and that you come to trust them for your holiday table.

WHAT: SHABBAT OR ROSH HASHANAH

WHEN: FRIDAY NIGHTS OR SEPTEMBER / OCTOBER

These nourishing, soulful classics are perfect for ending a long week or ringing in a new year.

CHALLAH 177
CHOPPED LIVER 45
CHICKEN SOUP with **KREPLACH** 151, 154
SPRING CHICKEN 143
BRUSSELS SPROUTS 161
KNISHES 165
HONEY CAKE 198

WHAT: PASSOVER

WHEN: MARCH / APRIL

Your guests will be so impressed with the housemade matzo, and they won't believe that the cake is *pesadik*. For the table, we love to place a pickled egg in salt water at each setting as a symbolic echo of the *beitzah* on the seder plate. It's also a great snack for those who need sustenance as they sit through the first part of the seder.

PICKLED EGGS 67
MATZO 187
CHICKEN SOUP with **MATZO BALLS** 151, 155
GEFILTE FISH with **CHRAIN** 60, 86
GOLDEN BEET SALAD WITH SCHMALTZ VINAIGRETTE 170
BRAISED BRISKET WITH RED WINE & PRUNES 140
TSIMIS 159
FLOURLESS CHOCOLATE CAKE 194

WHAT: **HANUKKAH PARTY**
WHEN: **NOVEMBER / DECEMBER**

Our favorite part of the winter holiday season is celebrating with a latke bar. It works just as well for a cocktail party as it does for a casual family gathering. Just set out the toppings and allow guests to mix and match their own.

LATKES 168, with toppings:

APPLESAUCE 80

HORSERADISH CREAM 90

LOX 56

Either serve slices of lox over a dollop of the Horseradish Cream, or dice up the

PICKLED BELLY LOX, 57

SMOKED WHITEFISH SALAD 108

PICKLED BEETS 72

Mix the diced beets into a salad with blue cheese.

If you prefer to go with a meat menu:

LAMB BACON 52, and fried egg

SCHMEAR OF CHOPPED LIVER 45,
  topped with **PICKLED RED ONIONS** 66

SMOKED MEAT 33, and mustard

Plus, don't forget the best way to partake in the commemoration of the miracle of oil:

JELLY DOUGHNUTS 208

OLIVE OIL CAKE with warm **COMPOTE** 195, 193

WHAT: **SHAVUOT**
WHEN: **MAY / JUNE**

On this holiday, which celebrates the day the Torah was given to the Jews at Mount Sinai, the tradition is to eat dairy foods. We could make a whole meal out of the blintzes, but for a more rounded menu, start with the veggie-heavy borscht. If you prefer a fish option that can be prepared in advance, just swap the trout for Smoked Whitefish Salad (page 108), and serve it with pumpernickel and a side of cream cheese.

PUMPERNICKEL BREAD 174

BORSCHT 157

PAN-SEARED TROUT 148

BLINTZES 110

CHEESECAKE 191

A MILE END FOOD TOUR

Montreal is, quite simply, one of the most energetic and vibrant cities in the world. Not particularly large or populous, it nonetheless possesses a sophisticated cosmopolitanism, replete with great artists, an experimental music scene, and, of course, pioneering chefs and restaurants. Best of all, visitors can experience the best Montreal has to offer at a fraction of the cost of visiting many of its rivals, namely New York, San Francisco, and Paris.

Montreal is home to one of the most innovative food scenes in North America, combining the city's rich multiculturalism, Francophone roots, and prized agriculture. Our favorite spots have little connection to cost and everything to do with quintessence: the coffee (and porch) at Club Social, the charred chicken at Rotisserie Romados, the Chilean grandmas making empanadas at Supermarché Andes. For those looking for maximum maximalism, visit our friends David McMillan and Frédéric Morin at Joe Beef and Liverpool House, or Martin Picard's game changers, Au Pied du Cochon and Cabane à Sucre. For those seeking the sources of inspiration for this book, we recommend a day on foot visiting the Yiddish institutions of the Mile End (opposite).